Nunc Loquāmur

Guided Conversations for Latin

SECOND EDITION

Nunc Loquāmur

Guided Conversations for Latin

SECOND EDITION

Thomas McCarthy

focus Publishing
R Pullins Co
Newburyport, MA

Nunc Loquāmur
© 2009 Thomas McCarthy

Focus Publishing/R. Pullins Company
PO Box 369
Newburyport MA 01950
www.focusbookstore.com

ISBN: 978-1-58510-323-2

Printed in the United States of America.

13 12 11 10 9 8 7 6 5 4

1014W

Nunc Loquamur

Guided Conversations For Latin

Second Edition

Thomas McCarthy

Table of Contents

Prō Omnibus

I first encountered guided conversations when I began teaching ESL in Japan in 1990. They have been an important part of my 'bag of tricks' ever since. Students consistently give high marks to these activities when asked for feedback. Guided conversations give students an opportunity to use the language they're learning in a safe and meaningful way. They're safe because there are few opportunities to make mistakes. They're meaningful because each conversation provides context. The illustrations also support understanding.

Nunc Loquamur is suitable for students in the first two years of Latin. The material is appropriate for ages ranging from Middle School to Adult. It can be used to supplement any textbook the teacher is currently using. It can enhance the oral component of your book or provide one where it is lacking.

Prō Magistrīs

Nunc Loquamur is designed for ease of use, both for the teacher and the student. Open the book to any page and you are presented with a complete unit. Looking at the lesson, both teachers and students will know immediately what to do, so there is little need for explanation.

Each lesson begins with a complete conversation with parts underlined. Next, there are four variations with substitutions provided. Students gradually are required to write out more and more of the conversation. Finally students are invited to write a new variation of the conversation. This is a good opportunity to review material your class is working with or for students to pursue their own imaginations.

Prō Discipulīs

Declining nouns, conjugating verbs and worrying about agreement were not my favorite activities in my school-years. That's why you won't find much of those here! I've done the best I could to make this "Plug and Play". Does that mean this book is a piece of cake? *Minime*! You will do a lot of writing, reading, speaking and listening. The final part of each lesson requires you to create a conversation in Latin. Are you hyperventilating? You can stop now. Change a noun here, a verb there and you'll be all set.

Acknowledgments

Robert Patrick encouraged me and tried this material first. Michelle Vitt (Minnehaha Academy) provided much-needed editing and welcome suggestions. Professor Jeanne Neumann (Davidson College) gave many suggestions and added polish for the second printing. Further emenda were found by Professor Akihiko Watanabe (Western Washington University) and Jacque Myers (St. Matthew's Parish School). Without their considerate effort, this book would not be possible.

New Features in the Second Edition

Audio files and software are freely available from the author's and publisher's websites. Besides extensive error correction, some new features have been added to enhance the usefulness of this book. Extra suggestion boxes have been added to some units and many more resources are listed in the appendix. Five additional units with a unified theme have been added to the end. A few appendices, such as grammar notes and activity ideas, have also been added.

Suggestions for using

1. Introduce the model dialogue. Play the CD or perform it with a student. (Audio files available for free download from the author's and publisher's websites.)

2. Briefly describe the grammatical features. Check out the new grammar notes appendix.

3. Instruct students to write out the four variations

4. Assign pairs of students to practice and perform a given dialogue. Encourage students to make eye contact when speaking. "Look down to read. Look up to speak."
   You may with to create pairs by calling on students randomly, e.g. "Richard, you're 'A'. Naomi, you're 'B'. Do dialogue 4." Richard and Naomi ideally are on different sides of the room.

5. Instruct students to create their own variations. This could also be done as homework. Encourage students to stretch their language. Invite drawing. Pictures can also be clipped from catalogues and magazines with dramatic results.

6. Students perform their own dialogues. A unique innovation of Nunc Loquamur is part 6. Students are asked to write out what another pair of students is saying. This encourages students to listen to each other. It can easily be organized by instructing pairs to fill in dialogue 6 with information from the pair that performs immediately following themselves. For example; pair A performs and sits. Pair B performs (pair A uses information from pair B to complete dialogue 6).

7. Mix and match. After mastering a few dialogues, ask students to combine two or three to make a longer presentation.

For more information please visit my websites: **www.perlingua.com** & **www.discamus.com**.

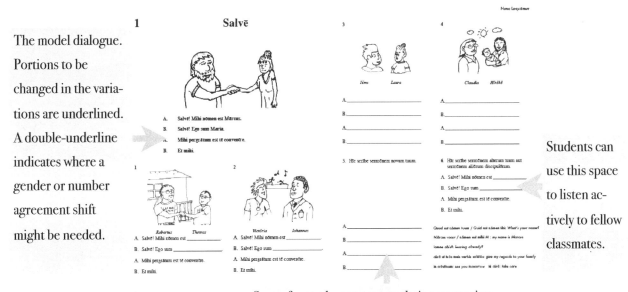

The model dialogue. Portions to be changed in the variations are underlined. A double-underline indicates where a gender or number agreement shift might be needed.

Students can use this space to listen actively to fellow classmates.

Space for students to create their own version.

1   **Salvē**

Stress on second syllable of two syllable word

A.   **Salvē! Mihi nōmen est <u>Mārcus</u>.**   Hello! My name is Marcus

B.   **Salvē! Ego sum <u>Maria</u>.**   Hello! I am Maria

A.   **Mihi pergrātum est tē convenīre.**   It is pleasure for me to meet you

B.   **Et mihi.**   and me

1

Robertus   *Thomas*

A. Salvē! Mihi nōmen est ___Robertus___ .

B. Salvē! Ego sum ___Thomas___ .

A. Mihi pergrātum est tē convenīre.

B. Et mihi.

2

Victōria   *Iohannes*

A. Salvē! Mihi nōmen est ___Victoria___ .

B. Salvē! Ego sum ___Iohannes___ .

A. Mihi pergrātum est tē convenīre.

B. Et mihi.

3

Iēms   *Laura*

A._____

B._____

A._____

B._____

4

Claudia   *Hīrōkō*

A._____

B._____

A._____

B._____

5. Hīc scrībe sermōnem novum tuum.

William: Salve Zachary! Quid agis?

Zachary: Salve william! valeo

William: Bene, gratias, Cura et tuos meis verbis salutes

Zachary: Et tu

William: Quid novi   Zachary: Thermae

Zachary: nullum glaus William: bonum iter

William: Quo tendis? Zachary: in posterum
William: vale!

A. Quid est nomen tibi

B. Nomen est mihi zachary

A. Quid agis?

B. Bene, gratias

6. Hīc scrībe sermōnem alterum tuum aut sermōnem aliōrum discipulōrum.

A. Salvē! Mihi nōmen est __William__.

B. Salvē! Ego sum __Zachary__.

A. Mihi pergrātum est tē convenīre.

B. Et mihi.

Quod est nōmen tuum / Quid est nōmen tibi:	What's your name?
Mārcus vocor / nōmen est mihi M :	my name is Marcus
Iamne abīs?:	leaving already?
cūrā ut tuōs meīs verbīs salūtēs:	give my regards to your family
in crāstīnum: see you tomorrow	tē cūrā: take care

2   Velim trādere tibi...

A.   **Salvē! Quid agis?**

B.   **Bene mihi est. Quid agis tū?**

A.   **Rēctē, grātiās. Velim trādere tibi <u>frātrem meum, Mārcum.</u>**

B.   **<u>Mārce</u>, mihi pergrātum est <u>tē</u> convenīre.**

1

amīcum meum, Robertum   *Roberte*

A. Salvē! Quid agis?

B. Bene mihi est. Quid agis tū?

A. Rēctē, grātiās. Velim trādere tibi

_____.

B. _____, mihi pergrātum est tē convenīre.

2

mātrem meam, Victōriam   *Victōria*

A. Salvē! Quid agis?

B. Bene mihi est. Quid agis tū?

A. Rēctē, grātiās. Velim trādere tibi

_____.

B. _____, mihi pergrātum est tē convenīre.

3

marītum meum, Ariovistum   *Arioviste*

A._____

B._____

A._____

B._____

_____

5. Hīc scrībe sermōnem novum tuum.

A._____

B._____

A._____

B._____

4

sorōrēs meās,   *Prīma et Secūnda*
Prīmam et Secūndam   *(vōs)*

A._____

B._____

A._____

B._____

_____

6. Hīc scrībe sermōnem alterum tuum aut sermōnem aliōrum discipulōrum.

A. Salvē! Quid agis?

B. Bene mihi est. Quid agis tū?

A. Rēctē, grātiās. Velim trādere tibi

_____.

B. _____, mihi pergrātum est tē con-venīre.

pa·ter -tris: *father*	**patru·us -ī:** *paternal uncle*
mā·ter -tris: *mother*	**avuncul·us -ī:** *maternal uncle*
frā·ter -tris: *brother*	**amit·a -ae:** *paternal aunt*
sor·or -ōris: *sister*	**māterter·a -ae:** *maternal aunt*
av·us -ī: *grandfather*	**ux·or -ōris:** *wife*
avi·a -ae: *grandmother*	**cognāt·us -ī:** *relative*

3   Quid est nōmen tibi?

A.   Quid est nōmen tibi?

B.   <u>Aurēlius.</u>

A.   Unde venīs?

B.   <u>Ītāliā.</u>

A.   Ō, <u>Rōmā</u> venīs?

B.   Nōn. <u>Ostiā.</u>

1

Robertus, Americā, Atlantā   Bostōniā?

A. Quid est nōmen tibi?

B. _____.

A. Unde venīs?

B. _____.

A. Ō, _____ venīs?

B. Nōn. _____.

2

Victōria, Germāniā,   Berolīnō?
Norinburgā

A. Quid est nōmen tibi?

B. _____.

A. Unde venīs?

B. _____.

A. Ō, _____ venīs?

B. Nōn. _____.

3

Iēms, Britanniā,   *Londoniō?*
  Cantabrigriā

A. _____

B. _____

A. _____

B. _____

A. _____

B. _____

5. Hīc scrībe sermōnem novum tuum.

4

Hīrōkō, Nīppōnicā, Ōsākā   *Tōkyōne?*

A. _____

B. _____

A. _____

B. _____

A. _____

B. _____

6. Hīc scrībe sermōnem alterum tuum aut sermōnem aliōrum discipulōrum.

A. _____

B. _____

A. _____

B. _____

A. _____

B. _____

A. Quid est nōmen tibi?

B. _____.

A. Unde venīs?

B. _____.

A. Ō, _____ venīs?

B. Nōn. _____.

4   Quid est praenōmen tibi?

A.   **Quid est praenōmen tibi?**

B.   **Mārcus.**

A.   **Quid est nōmen tibi?**

B.   **Aurēlius.**

A.   **Quot annōs nā<u>tus</u> es?**

B.   **<u>Octō et quīnquāgintā</u>.**

1

Mohandas, Gandhi, octō et septuāgintā

A. Quid est praenōmen tibi?

B. _____.

A. Quid est nōmen tibi?

B. _____.

A. Quot annōs nātus es?

B. _____.

2

Harrieta, Tubman, trēs et nōnāgintā

A. Quid est praenōmen tibi?

B. _____.

A. Quid est nōmen tibi?

B. _____.

A. Quot annōs nāta es?

B. _____.

3

XXXIX

Martīnus, Luther King Jr., novem et trīgintā

A._____

B._____

A._____

B._____

A._____

B._____

5. Hīc scrībe sermōnem novum tuum.

A._____

B._____

A._____

B._____

A._____

B._____

4

LVI

Abraham, Lincoln, sex et quīnquāgintā

A._____

B._____

A._____

B._____

A._____

B._____

6. Hīc scrībe sermōnem alterum tuum aut sermōnem aliōrum discipulōrum.

A. Quid est praenōmen tibi?

B. _____.

A. Quid est nōmen tibi?

B. _____.

A. Quot annōs nāt__ es?

B. _____.

I	unum	VI	sex	XI	ūndecim	XVI	sēdecim	XXX	trīgintā	LXXX	octōgintā
II	duo	VII	septem	XII	duodecim	XVII	septendecim	XL	quadrāgintā	XC	nōnāgintā
III	trēs	VIII	octō	XIII	tredecim	XVIII	duodēvīgintī	L	quīnquāgintā	C	centum
IV	quattuor	IX	novem	XIV	quattuordecim	IXX	ūndēvīgintī	LX	sexāgintā		
V	quīnque	X	decem	XV	quīndecim	XX	vīgintī	LXX	septuāgintā		

5   Esne cīvis Americāna?

A. Salvē! Mihi nōmen est <u>Mārcus Aurēlius</u>.

B. Salvē! Ego sum <u>Lydia Caesar</u>.

A. Esne cīvis <u>Americāna</u>?

B. Sīc. <u>Novō Eborācō</u> veniō. Et tū?

A. Cīvis <u>Rōmānus</u> sum. <u>Ostiā</u> veniō.

1

Maculōsus, Dalmatiānus, Spalātō
Albus, Afghanistānus, Kabūle

A. Salvē! Mihi nōmen est

_____.

B. Salvē! Ego sum _____.

A. Esne cīvis _____?

B. Sīc. _____ veniō. Et tū?

A. Cīvis _____ sum.

_____ veniō.

2

Hīrōko Ōnīshi, Nīppōnica, Ōsākā
Robertus Brown, Americānus, Geōrgiā

A. Salvē! Mihi nōmen est

_____.

B. Salvē! Ego sum _____.

A. Esne cīvis _____?

B. Sīc. _____ veniō. Et tū?

A. Cīvis _____ sum.

_____ veniō.

3

Mohammed al Sadat, Aegyptinus, Cairōne
Anna Miller, Austrāliānā, Melburneō

A._____

B._____

A._____

B._____

A._____

_____

5. Hīc scrībe sermōnem novum tuum.

A._____

B._____

A._____

B._____

A._____

_____

4

Selēna Panos, Graeca, Athenīs
Amēlia Henry, Hibernica, Dublinō

A._____

B._____

A._____

B._____

A._____

_____

6. Hīc scrībe sermōnem alterum tuum aut sermōnem aliōrum discipulōrum.

A. Salvē! Mihi nōmen est

_____.

B. Salvē! Ego sum _____.

A. Esne cīvis _____?

B. Sīc. _____ veniō. Et tū?

A. Cīvis _____ sum.

_____ veniō.

6   Numerum falsum

A. Salvē.

B. Salvē! <u>Mārce?</u>

A. Fortasse numerum falsum habēs.

B. Estne <u>882-6780?</u>

A. Nōn.

B. Ō. Ignōsce mihi.

0	zerum / nihil	5	quīnque
1	unum	6	sex
2	duo	7	septem
3	tria	8	octō
4	quattuor	9	novem

1

A. Salvē.

B. Salvē! _____?

A. Fortasse numerum falsum habēs.

B. Estne _____?

A. Nōn.

B. Ō. Ignōsce mihi.

2

A. Salvē.

B. Salvē! _____?

A. Fortasse numerum falsum habēs.

B. Estne _____?

A. Nōn.

B. Ō. Ignōsce mihi.

3

Laura?
501-2833?

4

Mohammed?
772-9460?

A._____

B._____

A._____

B._____

A._____

B._____

A._____

B._____

A._____

B._____

A._____

B._____

5. Hīc scrībe sermōnem novum tuum.

6. Hīc scrībe sermōnem alterum tuum aut sermōnem aliōrum discipulōrum.

A._____

B._____

A._____

B._____

A._____

B.._____

A. Salvē.

B. Salvē! _____?

A. Fortasse numerum falsum habēs.

B. Estne _____?

A. Nōn.

B. Ō. Ignōsce mihi.

7   Adestne Mārcus illīc?

A.   **Salvē.**

B.   **Salvē! Adestne <u>Mārcus</u> illīc?**

A.   **Nōn adest. Nunc <u>in lūdō</u> est.**

B.   **Intellegō. Iterum telephonicē vocābō.**

A.   **Valē.**

1

in argentāriā

A. Salvē.

B. Salvē! Adestne _____ illīc?

A. Nōn adest.

   Nunc _____ est.

B. Intellegō. Iterum telephonicē vocābō.

A. Valē.

2

in tabernā vestiāriā

A. Salvē.

B. Salvē! Adestne _____ illīc?

A. Nōn adest.

   Nunc _____ est.

B. Intellegō. Iterum telephonicē vocābō.

A. Valē.

3

in stadiō

A._____

B._____

A._____

B._____

A._____

5. Hīc scrībe sermōnem novum tuum.

A._____

B._____

A._____

B._____

A._____

4

in pīstrīnā

A._____

B._____

A._____

B._____

A._____

6. Hīc scrībe sermōnem alterum tuum aut sermōnem aliōrum discipulōrum.

A. Salvē.

B. Salvē! Adestne _____ illīc?

A. Nōn adest.
   Nunc _____ est.

B. Intellegō. Iterum telephonicē vocābō.

A. Valē.

8   Nunc occupātus sum.

   A.   **Mārce? Quid agis?**

   B.   **Bene, sed nunc occupātus sum.**

           Cubiculum purgō.

   A.   **Ō. Ignōsce mihi.**

   B.   **Nōlī sollicitāri. Posteā tē tēlephōnicē vocābō.**

   A.   **Bene. Valeās.**

1

Julī   *Bellum gerō*

A. _____? Quid agis?

B. Bene, sed nunc occupātus sum.

_____.

A. Ō. Ignōsce mihi.

B. Nōlī sollicitārī.
Posteā tē tēlephōnicē vocābō.

A. Bene. Valeās.

2

Phaëthon   *Sōlum per aerēs trahō*

A. _____? Quid agis?

B. Bene, sed nunc occupātus sum.

_____.

A. Ō. Ignōsce mihi.

B. Nōlī sollicitārī.
Posteā tē tēlephōnicē vocābō.

A. Bene. Valeās.

3

Tullī   *Rem pūblicam servō*

A._____

B._____

_____

A._____

B._____

A._____

5. Hīc scrībe sermōnem novum tuum.

A._____

B._____

_____

A._____

B._____

A._____

4

Apollō   *Puellam petō*

A._____

B._____

_____

A._____

B._____

6. Hīc scrībe sermōnem alterum tuum aut sermōnem aliōrum discipulōrum.

A. _____? Quid agis?

B. Bene, sed nunc occupā____ sum.

_____.

A. Ō. Ignōsce mihi.

B. Nōlī sollicitārī.
Posteā tē tēlephōnicē vocābō.

A. Bene. Valeās.

9   Quota hōra est?

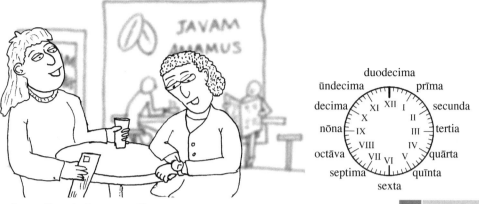

A.   **Quota hōra est?**

B.   <u>**Quārta hōra.**</u>

A.   **Ō! Mihi eundum est. Opus est mihi <u>litterās dāre</u>.**

B.   **Bene. Iterum conveniāmus.**

1

domum redīre   *tertia*

A.   Quota hōra est?

B.   _____ hōra.

A.   Ō! Mihi eundum est. Opus est mihi

    _____.

B.   Bene. Iterum conveniāmus.

2

librum bibliothēcae reddere   *tertia et dīmidia*

A.   Quota hōra est?

B.   _____ hōra.

A.   Ō! Mihi eundum est. Opus est mihi

    _____.

B.   Bene. Iterum conveniāmus.

3

pānem emere

A._____

B._____

A._____

_____

B._____

5. Hīc scrībe sermōnem novum tuum.

A._____

B._____

A._____

_____

B._____

4

cēnam coquere

A._____

B._____

A._____

_____

B._____

6. Hīc scrībe sermōnem alterum tuum aut sermōnem aliōrum discipulōrum.

A. Quota hōra est?

B. _____ hōra.

A. Ō! Mihi eundum est. Opus est mihi

_____.

B. Bene. Iterum conveniāmus.

10   Quotā hōrā incipiet?

A.   Quotā hōrā <u>bellum Germānicum</u> incipiet?

B.   <u>Secundā hōrā.</u>

A.   Quid! Tantum <u>quīnque</u> minūtae rémanent.

B.   Nōbīs festīnandum est!

1   **2**

Ōrātio Cicerōnis,   *prīmā et dīmidiā*   *Circus,*   *Hodiē māne nōnā*
quīndecim   *quīnque et vīgintī*

A.   Quotā hōrā _____   A.   Quotā hōrā _____

     _____incipiet?   _____incipiet?

B.   _____ hōrā.   B.   _____ hōrā.

A.   Quid! Tantum _____   A.   Quid! Tantum _____

     minūtae rémanent.   minūtae rémanent.

B.   Nōbīs festīnandum est!   B.   Nōbīs festīnandum est!

3

cēna apud Catullum,   *quīntā*
vīgintī

A._____

    _____

B._____

A._____

    _____

B._____

5. Hīc scrībe sermōnem novum tuum.

A._____

    _____

B._____

A._____

    _____

B._____

4

pellicula, decem   *tertiā*

A._____

    _____

B._____

A._____

    _____

B._____

6. Hīc scrībe sermōnem alterum tuum aut sermōnem aliōrum discipulōrum.

A. Quotā hōrā _____

    _____incipiet?

B. _____ hōrā.

A. Quid! Tantum _____

    minūtae rémanent.

B. Nōbīs festīnandum est!

11   Possumne tibi aliquid emere?

A.   Ad macellum eō ut <u>māla</u> emam. Possumne tibi aliquid emere?

B.   Etiam. <u>Pira</u> emās, quaesō.

A.   <u>Quot</u>?

B.   <u>Duo aut tria</u> satis putō.

1

A. vīnum, Quantum?
B. fabās cafēae, duo aut tria chiliográmmata

A.   Ad macellum eō ut _____

emam. Possumne tibi aliquid emere?

B.   Etiam. _____ emās, quaesō.

A.   _____?

B.   _____ satis putō.

2

A. oleum, Quantum?
B. lāc, ūnam aut duās ampullās

A.   Ad macellum eō ut _____

emam. Possumne tibi aliquid emere?

B.   Etiam. _____ emās, quaesō.

A.   _____?

B.   _____ satis putō.

3

A. *piscēs, Quot?*
B. *pānēs, quattuor aut quīnque*

A. _____

_____

B. _____

A. _____

B. _____

5. Hīc scrībe sermōnem novum tuum.

A. _____

_____

B. _____

A. _____

B. _____

săcc•um -ī: *bag*	fasc•is -is m: *package*
lītr•a -ae: *liter*	sextāri•us -ī: *pint*
arc•a -ae: *box*	chiliogram•ma -matis: *kg*

4

A. *carnem, Quantum?*
B. *sanguinem, trēs aut quattuor ampullās*

A. _____

_____

B. _____

A. _____

B. _____

6. Hīc scrībe sermōnem alterum tuum aut sermōnem aliōrum discipulōrum.

A. Ad macellum eō ut _____ emam. Possumne tibi aliquid emere?

B. Etiam. _____ emās, quaesō.

A. _____?

B. _____ satis putō.

cāse•us -ī: *cheese*	cereal•is -is m: *cereal*
crūstul•um -ī: *cookie*	acēt•um - ī: *vinegar*
lāminae solānōrum (fpl): *potato chips*	

27

12   Quō īs?

A.   **Salvē! Quid agis?**

B.   **Bellē. Et tū?**

A.   **Mē bene habeō. Quō īs?**

B.   <u>**Ad stadium**</u>**. Et tū?**

A.   <u>**Ad forum**</u>**. Numquid vīs?**

B.   **Ut valeās.**

1   **2**

ad tōnstrīnam   *Domum*   *ad theātrum*   *ad librāriam*

A.   Salvē! Quid agis?   A.   Salvē! Quid agis?

B.   Bellē. Et tū?   B.   Bellē. Et tū?

A.   Mē bene habeō. Quō īs?   A.   Mē bene habeō. Quō īs?

B. _____. Et tū?   B. _____. Et tū?

A. _____. Numquid vīs?   A. _____. Numquid vīs?

B.   Ut valeās.   B.   Ut valeās.

3

ad tabernam flōrālem   *ad gymnasium*

A. _____

B. _____

A. _____

B. _____

A. _____

B. _____

5. Hīc scrībe sermōnem novum tuum.

A. _____

B. _____

A. _____

B. _____

A. _____

B. _____

4

ad thermās   *ad lūdum*

A. _____

B. _____

A. _____

B. _____

A. _____

B. _____

6. Hīc scrībe sermōnem alterum tuum aut sermōnem aliōrum discipulōrum.

A. Salvē! Quid agis?
B. Bellē. Et tū?
A. Mē bene habeō. Quō īs?
B. _____. Et tū?

A. _____. Numquid vīs?
B. Ut valeās.

medicāmentāri·a, ae: *drug store*	**lani·us -ī:** *butcher shop*
cuppedināri·a -ae: *pastry shop*	**campus Ēlysius:** *paradise*
macell·um -ī: *grocery store*	**Tartar·a -ōrum:** *the underworld*
meschīt·a -ae: *mosque*	**iūdici·um -ī:** *court, trial*
synagōg·a -ae: *synagogue*	**ecclēsi·a -ae:** *church*

13   Licetne mihi...

A.   **Licetne mihi aliquid rogāre?**

B.   **Quippe.**

A.   **Licetne mihi <u>lūdere</u>?**

B.   **Licet / Nōn licet.**

1

cras pēnsum trādere

A.   Licetne mihi aliquid rogāre?

B.   Quippe.

A.   Licetne mihi _____

_____ ?

B.   Licet / Nōn licet.

2

scrīptūram meam per litterās ēlectronicās dāre

A.   Licetne mihi aliquid rogāre?

B.   Quippe.

A.   Licetne mihi _____

_____ ?

B.   Licet / Nōn licet.

3

graphidem cuspidāre

A. _____

B. _____

A. _____

   _____

B. _____

4

tēlevīsiōnem spectāre

A. _____

B. _____

A. _____

   _____

B. _____

5. Hīc scrībe sermōnem novum tuum.

A. _____

B. _____

A. _____

   _____

B. _____

6. Hīc scrībe sermōnem alterum tuum aut sermōnem aliōrum discipulōrum.

A. Licetne mihi aliquid rogāre?

B. Quippe.

A. Licetne mihi _____

   _____?

B. Licet / Nōn licet.

ad locum sēcrētum īre: *to go to the lavatory*
ad loculamentum (*aut* capsam) īre: *to go to my locker*
nōtīs meīs inter probātiōnem ūtī: *to use my notes in the test*
dulciolum in conclāve edere (ēsse): *to eat candy in class*
mātūrē domum redīre: *to go home early*

31

14   Ubi est argentāria?

A.   Ignōsce mihi. Ubi est <u>argentāria</u>?

B.   <u>Argentāria</u>? Est <u>iūxtā pīstrīnam</u>.

A.   <u>Iūxtā pīstrīnam</u>?

B.   Itast.

A.   Grātiās.

B.   Libenter.

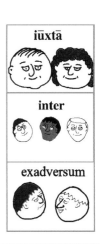

iūxtā

inter

exadversum

itast = ita est

1

pīstrīna   bibliothēcam

A. Ignōsce mihi. Ubi est _____?

B. _____? Est_____

_____.

A. _____?

B. Itast.

A. Grātiās.

B. Libenter.

2

bibliothēca   *aedem cursuālem et
dēversōrium*

A. Ignōsce mihi. Ubi est _____?

B. _____? Est_____

_____.

A. _____?

B. Itast.

A. Grātiās.

B. Libenter.

3

aedes cursuālis   *popīnam*

A. _____

B. _____

_____

A. _____

B. _____

A. _____

B. _____

5. Hīc scrībe sermōnem novum tuum.

A. _____

B. _____

_____

A. _____

B. _____

A. _____

B. _____

4

popīna   *pīstrīnam et valētūdinārium*

A. _____

B. _____

_____

A. _____

B. _____

A. _____

B. _____

6. Hīc scrībe sermōnem alterum tuum aut sermōnem aliōrum discipulōrum.

A. Ignōsce mihi. Ubi est _____?

B. _____?

Est _____.

A. _____?

B. Itast.

A. Grātiās.

B. Libenter.

15   Vīdistīne galeam meam?

     A.   Vīdistīne <u>galeam meam</u>?

     B.   <u>Estne haec tua</u>?

     A.   Nōn. <u>Ista est</u> <u>antīqua</u>. <u>Mea est</u> <u>nova</u>.

     B.   Ō. <u>Galea tua est</u> in mediānō.

1

canem meum,
magnus, parvus   *in hortō*

A. Vīdistīne _____?

B. Estne hic tuus?

A. Nōn. Iste est _____.

     _____ est_____.

B. Ō. _____tuus est _____.

2

librum meum,
Mathēmaticus, Latīnus   *in locō sēcrētō*

A. Vīdistīne _____?

B. Estne hic tuus?

A. Nōn. Iste est _____.

     _____ est_____.

B. Ō. _____tuus est _____.

3

fīlius meus,   *in cubiculō*
probus, improbus   *magistrī summō*

A. _____

B. _____

A. _____

_____

B. _____

5. Hīc scrībe sermōnem novum tuum.

A. _____

B. _____

A. _____

_____

B. _____

4

caput meum,
simile mōnstrō, simile pepōnī   *sub ponte*

A. _____

B. _____

A. _____

_____

B. _____

6. Hīc scrībe sermōnem alterum tuum aut sermōnem aliōrum discipulōrum.

A. Vīdistīne _____?

B. Estne h_____ tu_____?

A. Nōn. Ist__ est _____.

_____ est_____.

B. Ō. _____tu_____ est _____

16 Possumne tibi ministrāre?

A. **Salvē, dominę.**

   Possumne tibi ministrāre?

B. **Potes. Opus est mihi <u>togā</u>.**

A. **<u>Togae</u> sunt illīc.**

B. **Grātiās.**

1

stolae   *stolā*

A. Salvē, domina.

   Possumne tibi ministrāre?

B. Potes. Opus est mihi _____.

A. _____ sunt illīc.

B. Grātiās.

2

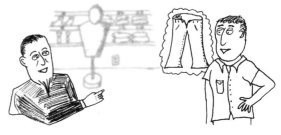

brācae   *brācīs*

A. Salvē, domine.

   Possumne tibi ministrāre?

B. Potes. Opus est mihi _____.

A. _____ sunt illīc.

B. Grātiās.

3

cingula   *cingulō*

A._____

_____

B._____

_____

A._____

B._____

4

lūsūs computātrālēs   *lūsū computātrālī*

A._____

_____

B._____

_____

A._____

B._____

5. Hīc scrībe sermōnem novum tuum.

A._____

_____

B._____

_____

A._____

B._____

6. Hīc scrībe sermōnem alterum tuum aut sermōnem aliōrum discipulōrum.

A. Salvē, domin___.

Possumne tibi ministrāre?

B. Potes. Opus est mihi _____.

A. _____ sunt illīc.

B. Grātiās.

calce•us -ī: *a shoe*	focāl•e -is: *a necktie*
ānul•us -ī: *a ring*	pup•a -ae: *a doll*
pétas•us -ī: *a hat*	lūdiment•um -ī: *a toy*
hōrolōgium bracchiāle: *a wristwatch*	
capsula scholastica: *a school bag*	

17   Quantī illa toga cōnstat?

A.   Quantī <u>illa</u> <u>toga</u> cōnsta<u>t</u>?

B.   <u>Haec</u> <u>toga</u> <u>vīgintī</u> dollarīs cōnsta<u>t</u>.

A.   Ostende mihi <u>illam</u>.

B.   Ecce.

A.   Satis. Emam.

1

quīnquāgintā   *stola*

A. Quantī ill__ _____ cōnstat?

B. H_____ _____ _____

    dollarīs cōnstat.

A. Ostende mihi ill_____.

B. Ecce.

A. Satis. Emam.

2

sexāgintā   *(illae) brācae (cōnstant)*

A. Quantī ill__ _____ cōnsta___?

B. H_____ _____ _____

    dollarīs cōnsta___.

A. Ostende mihi ill_____.

B. Ecce.

A. Satis. Emam.

3

quīnque et trīgintā   *cingulum*

A. _____

B._____

_____

A. _____

B. _____

A. _____

4

duodēvīgintī   *lūsus computātrālis*

A. _____

B._____

_____

A. _____

B. _____

A. _____

5. Hīc scrībe sermōnem novum tuum.

A. _____

B._____

_____

A. _____

B. _____

A. _____

6. Hīc scrībe sermōnem alterum tuum aut sermōnem aliōrum discipulōrum.

A. Quantī ill__ _____ cōnsta___?

B. H_____ _____ _____

dollarīs cōnsta___.

A. Ostende mihi ill_____.

B. Ecce.

A. Satis. Emam.

vīl·is -is -e: *cheap*	mercimōni·um -ī: *a bargain*
(per)cār·us -a -um: *(very) expensive*	
Ostende mihi alter·um -am: *Show me another*	

18   Ista est optima!

A.   Vidē! Nov**am** **autoraedam** habeō. Quid cēnsēs?

B.   Babae! Ist**a** **est** optima.

A.   Grātiās. Laetissim**us** sum.

1

stolam   *pulchra*

A. Vidē!

Nov___ _____ habeō.

Quid cēnsēs?

B. Babae! Ist__ est _____.

A. Grātiās. Laetissim____ sum.

2

brācae   *iūcundae*

A. Vidē!

Nov___ _____ habeō.

Quid cēnsēs?

B. Babae! Ist__ ____ _____.

A. Grātiās. Laetissim____ sum.

3

Novum cingulum   *Istud est bellum*

A. _____!

_____

_____

B. _____

A. _____

5. Hīc scrībe sermōnem novum tuum.

A. _____!

_____

_____

B. _____

A. _____

4

Novum lūsum computātrālem   *Iste est mīrificus*

A. _____!

_____

_____

B. _____

A. _____

6. Hīc scrībe sermōnem alterum tuum aut sermōnem aliōrum discipulōrum.

A. Vidē!

Nov___ _____ habeō.

Quid cēnsēs?

B. Babae! Ist__ ____ _____.

A. Grātiās. Laetissim____ sum.

(per)bon·us -a -um: *(very) cool*	epic·us -a -um: *epic*
ēlegans -tis /urbān·us -a -um: *elegant*	
Habeō eundem / eandem / idem : *I have the same.*	

19   Calētur hodiē.

A.   <u>Calētur</u> hodiē. Vīsne <u>natāre in lacū</u>?

B.   Bonum cōnsilium! <u>Natēmus</u>.

1

Ningit, forīs lūdere   *lūdāmus*

A. _____ hodiē.

    Vīsne _____?

B. Bonum cōnsilium!

    _____.

2

Pluit, pelliculam spectāre   *spectēmus*

A. _____ hodiē.

    Vīsne _____?

B. Bonum cōnsilium!

    _____.

3

Sūdum est,
per hortōs dēambulāre   *dēambulēmus*

A. _____

    _____

B. _____

    _____

4

Ventōsum est, nāvigāre   *nāvigēmus*

A. _____

    _____

B. _____

    _____

5. Hīc scrībe sermōnem novum tuum.

A. _____

    _____

B. _____

    _____

6. Hīc scrībe sermōnem alterum tuum aut sermōnem aliōrum discipulōrum.

A. _____ hodiē.

    Vīsne _____?

B. Bonum cōnsilium!

    _____.

Quaenam est tempestās hodiē?			Quō gradū stat temperātūra?	
Sol	serēnum	pluit, -ere, pluit		calētur
	nūbilōsum	ningit, -ere, nīnxit		tepidum
Dubium est caelum : *The weather is uncertain.*				frīgidum
Tempestās abiit : *The storm has passed.*				
Āēr ūmidus est et crassus : *The air is sticky and heavy.*				

43

20   Aliquid ūnā agēmus?

A.   **Aliquid ūnā agēmus hodiē?**

B.   **Bene. <u>In lacū natēmus.</u>**

A.   **Em, abhinc hebdomadem ūnam <u>in lacū natāvimus.</u>**

       Vīsne <u>currere per hortōs?</u>

B.   **Bene. <u>Currāmus.</u>**

1	**2**

A. forīs lūsimus *B. forīs lūdāmus* * ad forum īre* *eāmus*	*A. pelliculam spectāvimus* *B. pelliculam spectēmus* * pila lūdere* *Pila lūdāmus*
A. Aliquid ūnā agēmus hodiē?	A. Aliquid ūnā agēmus hodiē?
B. Bene. _____.	B. Bene. _____.
A. Em. abhinc hebdomadem ūnam	A. Em. abhinc hebdomadem ūnam
_____.	_____.
Vīsne _____?	Vīsne _____?
B. Bene. _____.	B. Bene. _____.

3

dēambulāvimus
saltāre

per hortōs dēambulēmus
saltēmus

A. _____

B. _____

A. _____

_____

_____

B. _____

5. Hīc scrībe sermōnem novum tuum.

A. _____

B. _____

A. _____

_____

_____

B. _____

4

nāvigāvimus
piscātum īre

nāvigēmus
eāmus

A. _____

B. _____

A. _____

_____

_____

B. _____

6. Hīc scrībe sermōnem alterum tuum aut sermōnem aliōrum discipulōrum.

A. Aliquid ūnā faciēmus hodiē?

B. Bene. _____.

A. Em. abhinc hebdomadem ūnam

_____.

Vīsne _____?

B. Bene. _____.

21   In theātrō eram.

A.   Hāc nocte tēlephōnicē vocāvī, sed abfuistī.

B.   Etiam. <u>In theātrō eram.</u>

A.   Quid cēnsuistī?

B.   <u>Bonum erat.</u>

1

In forō cum amīcīs, Iūcundum erat

A.   Hāc nocte tēlephōnicē vocāvī, sed ab-

     fuistī.

B.   Etiam. _____ eram.

A.   Quid cēnsuistī?

B.   _____ .

2

In carcere, Malum erat

A.   Hāc nocte tēlephōnicē vocāvī, sed ab-

     fuistī.

B.   Etiam. _____ eram.

A.   Quid cēnsuistī?

B.   _____

3

In cūriā, Clāmōsa erat

A._____

_____

B. _____

A. _____

B. _____

4

In amphitheātrō, Ah, etiamnunc vīvō

A._____

_____

B. _____

A. _____

B. _____

5. Hīc scrībe sermōnem novum tuum.

A._____

_____

B. _____

A. _____

B. _____

6. Hīc scrībe sermōnem alterum tuum aut sermōnem aliōrum discipulōrum.

A. Hāc nocte tēlephōnicē vocāvī,

sed abfuistī.

B. Etiam. _____ eram.

A. Quid censuistī?

B. _____

22   Quid agēs crās?

A.   **Quid agēs crās?**

B.   <u>**Ad forum emptum ībō**</u>. **Et tū?**

A.   <u>**Ad merīdiem dormiam**</u>.

1   **2**

Cum amīcō lūdam   *Cubiculum purgābō*

Ad lītus ībō   *Aliquās litterās ēlectronicās amīcīs dābō*

A. Quid agēs crās?   A. Quid agēs crās?

B. _____. Et tū?   B. _____. Et tū?

A. _____.   A. _____

3

Pedifolle lūdam   *Notās meās prō probātiōne ēdiscam*

A. _____

B. _____

A. _____

4

Aviam vīsitābō   *Birotam resarciam*

A. _____

B. _____

A. _____

5. Hīc scrībe sermōnem novum tuum.

A. _____

B. _____

A. _____

6. Hīc scrībe sermōnem alterum tuum aut sermōnem aliōrum discipulōrum.

A. Quid agēs crās?

B. _____. Et tū?

A. _____

chartulīs lūdere: *to play cards*	in cīnēmatēum īre: *to go to the movies*
cītherā canere: *to play the guitar*	pēnsa domestica facere: *to do chores*
vēn·or -ārī: *to hunt*	scrīptūram compōnere: *to write an essay*
forīs cēnāre: *to dine out*	pecūniam quaerere: *to look for money*
continentem reperīre: *to discover a continent*	philosoph·or -ārī: *to philosophize*
domī mihi manendum est / necesse est mihi domī manēre: *I have to stay home*	

49

23   Quid herī ēgistī?

A.   **Quid herī ēgistī?**

B.   <u>**Ad forum emptum īvī.**</u>

A.   **Bonum vidētur.**

B.   **Bonum erat. Et tū?**

A.   <u>**Ad merīdiem dormīvī.**</u>

1

Cum amīcō lūsī   *Cubiculum purgāvī*

2

Ad lītus īvī   *Aliquās litterās ēlectronicās amīcīs dēdī*

A. Quid herī ēgistī?

B. _____.

A. Bonum vidētur.

B. Bonum erat. Et tū?

A. _____.

A. Quid herī ēgistī?

B. _____.

A. Bonum vidētur.

B. Bonum erat. Et tū?

A. _____.

3

Pedifolle lūsī   *Notās meās
prō probātiōne ēdidicī*

A. _____
B. _____
A. _____
B. _____
A. _____

4

Aviam vīsitāvī   *Birotam resarsī*

A. _____
B. _____
A. _____
B. _____
A. _____

5. Hīc scrībe sermōnem novum tuum.

A. _____
B. _____
A. _____
B. _____
A. _____

6. Hīc scrībe sermōnem alterum tuum aut sermōnem aliōrum discipulōrum.

A. Quid herī ēgistī?
B. _____.
A. Bonum vidētur.
B. Bonum erat. Et tū?
A. _____.

24   Nōn salvus sum.

A.   **Nōn salv<u>us</u> sum.**

B.   **Quid est tibi?**

A.   <u>**Caput mihi dolet**</u>.

B.   **Cūrā ut valeās.**

1

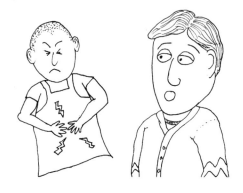

Stomachus mihi dolet

A. Nōn salv_____ sum.

B. Quid est tibi?

A. _____

B. Cūrā ut valeās.

2

Tussiō

A. Nōn salv_____ sum.

B. Quid est tibi?

A. _____

B. Cūrā ut valeās.

3

Febriō

A. _____

B. _____

A. _____

B. _____

5. Hīc scrībe sermōnem novum tuum.

A. _____

B. _____

A. _____

B. _____

4

Gravēdine labōrō

A. _____

B. _____

A. _____

B. _____

6. Hīc scrībe sermōnem alterum tuum aut sermōnem aliōrum discipulōrum.

A. Nōn salv_____ sum.

B. Quid est tibi?

A. _____

B. Cūrā ut valeās.

(in malīs) aeg·er -ra sum: *I am (terribly) ill.*	**cancrō labōrō:** *I suffer from cancer.*
Crūdō stomachō labōrō: *I have indigestion.*	**faucēs meae sunt raucae:** *I have a sore throat.*
est mihi crūs fractum: *I have a broken leg.*	**angīnā pectoris labōrō:** *I have a chest pain.*

25   Tū īrāta vidēris.

A.   Tū <u>īrāta</u> vidēris.

B.   Plānē. <u>Īrāta</u> sum.

A.   Quam ob rem?

B.   Quod <u>discipulī meī pēnsa nōn cōnficiunt</u>!

1   **2**

A. laetus   *B. crās erit diēs Sāturnī*   *A. tristis*   *B. canis meus est mortuus*

A. Tū _____ vidēris.   A. Tū _____ vidēris.

B. Plānē. _____ sum.   B. Plānē. _____ sum.

A. Quam ob rem?   A. Quam ob rem?

B. Quod _____!   B. Quod _____!

3

A. *sollicitus*   B. *crās erit probātiō Latīna*

A. _____

B. _____

A. _____

B. _____

4

A. *timidus*   B. *iamiamque post tē umbram vīdī*

A. _____

B. _____

A. _____

B. _____

5. Hīc scrībe sermōnem novum tuum.

A. _____

B. _____

A. _____

B. _____

6. Hīc scrībe sermōnem alterum tuum aut sermōnem aliōrum discipulōrum.

A. Tū _____ vidēris.

B. Plānē. _____ sum.

A. Quam ob rem?

B. Quod _____!

glōriōs·us -a -um: *proud*	invid·us -a -um: *envious*	dēlīr·us -a -um: *crazy*
dēspērāt·us -a -um: *desperate*	maest·us -a -um: *gloomy*	fess·us -a -um: *tired*
suspic·āx (-ācis): *suspicious*	loqu·āx (-ācis): *talkative*	taciturn·us -a -um: *quiet*

26   Māvīsne māla an pira?

A.   Māvīsne <u>māla an pira</u>?

B.   <u>Māla</u> mālō. Et tū?

A.   Ego <u>pira</u>.

1

fēlēs an canēs

A. Māvīsne _____?

B. _____ mālō. Et tū?

A. Ego _____.

2

aestātem an hiemem

A. Māvīsne _____?

B. _____ mālō. Et tū?

A. Ego _____.

3

librōs legere an litterās scrībere

A. _____

B. _____

A. _____

4

mūsicam audīre an pelliculam spectāre

A. _____

B. _____

A. _____

5. Hīc scrībe sermōnem novum tuum.

A. _____

B. _____

A. _____

6. Hīc scrībe sermōnem alterum tuum aut sermōnem aliōrum discipulōrum.

A. Māvīsne _____?

B. _____ mālō. Et tū?

A. Ego _____.

27   Quid tē hodiē dēlectet?

A.   **Quid tē hodiē dēlectet?**

B.   <u>**Isicium Hamburgense et solāna frīcta.**</u>

A.   **Aliquam pōtiōnem?**

B.   <u>**Coca-cōlam.**</u>

A.   **Edāsne hīc an forīs?**

B.   **Forīs / Hīc.**

1

rēticulatās et farcīmina, cafēam

A. Quid tē hodiē dēlectet?

B. _____ .

A. Aliquam pōtiōnem?

B. _____ .

A. Edāsne hīc an forīs?

B. _____ .

2

collȳrās et acētāria, theam

A. Quid tē hodiē dēlectet?

B. _____ .

A. Aliquam pōtiōnem?

B. _____ .

A. Edāsne hīc an forīs?

B. _____ .

3

būbulam assam, lāc

A. _____

B. _____

A. _____

B. _____

A. _____

B. _____

5. Hīc scrībe sermōnem novum tuum.

A. _____

B. _____

A. _____

B. _____

A. _____

B. _____

4

ōva frīcta et lardum, aurantiī pōtiōnem

A. _____

B. _____

A. _____

B. _____

A. _____

B. _____

6. Hīc scrībe sermōnem alterum tuum aut sermōnem aliōrum discipulōrum.

A. Quid tē hodiē dēlectet?

B. _____.

A. Aliquam pōtiōnem?

B. _____.

A. Edāsne hīc an forīs?

B. _____.

28   Illīc est domus mea.

A. Illīc est <u>domus</u> <u>mea</u>.

B. <u>Quaenam</u>?

A. <u>Illa</u> est <u>albā iānuā</u>.

B. Et <u>duābus fenestrīs</u>?

A. Sīc.

1

māter   *Quaenam*
longā stolā   *caeruleō petasō*

A. Illīc est _____ me___.

B. _____?

A. Ill__ est _____.

B. Et _____?

A. Sīc.

2

computātrum   *Quodnam*
iūxtā antīquuā impressōrium   *infractō monitōriō*

A. Illīc est _____ me___.

B. _____?

A. Ill__ est _____.

B. Et _____?

A. Sīc.

3

*liber,
iūcundīs pictūrīs*   *Quisnam
mōnstruōsīs sermōnibus*

A. _____

B. _____

A. _____

B. _____

A. _____

4

*homo
oculīs duōbus*   *Quisnam
ūnō nāsō*

A. _____

B. _____

A. _____

B. _____

A. _____

5. Hīc scrībe sermōnem novum tuum.

6. Hīc scrībe sermōnem alterum tuum aut sermōnem aliōrum discipulōrum.

A. _____

B. _____

A. _____

B. _____

A. _____

A. Illīc est _____ me___.

B. _____?

A. Ill__ est _____.

B. Et _____?

A. Sīc.

29 Ūterisne interrēte?

A.   Ūterisne interrēte?

B.   Ūtor. Cūr?

A.   Dā mihi, sōdēs, litterās ēlectronicās dē <u>hodiernō pēnsō</u>.

B.   Libenter. Quam inscriptiōnem ēlectronicam habēs?

A.   Mea est <u>mārcus@SPQR.gov</u>.

1

crastinā probātiōne, maria@studēbō.com

A. Ūterisne interrēte?

B. Ūtor. Cūr?

A. Dā mihi, sōdēs, litterās ēlectronicās dē

_____.

B. Libenter. Quam inscriptiōnem ēlectroni-cam habēs?

A. Mea est _____.

2

pugnā cum barbarīs, metuēns@fugiō.com

A. Ūterisne interrēte?

B. Ūtor. Cūr?

A. Dā mihi, sōdēs, litterās ēlectronicās dē

_____.

B. Libenter. Quam inscriptiōnem ēlectroni-cam habēs?

A. Mea est _____.

3

quō manipulō lūsum vīcerit,
egoeō@nōnvideō.com

A. _____

B. _____

A. _____

_____

B. _____

_____

A. _____

5. Hīc scrībe sermōnem novum tuum.

A. _____

B. _____

A. _____

_____

B. _____

_____

A. _____

4

quōmodo haec cēna parētur,
novissimus@coquus.com

A. _____

B. _____

A. _____

_____

B. _____

_____

A. _____

6. Hīc scrībe sermōnem alterum tuum aut sermōnem aliōrum discipulōrum.

A. Ūterisne interrēte?

B. Ūtor. Cūr?

A. Dā mihi, sōdēs, litterās ēlectronicās dē

_____.

B. Libenter. Quam inscriptiōnem ēlectroni-cam habēs?

A. Mea est _____.

@ = apud	. = punctum

A 'ā'	B 'bē'	C 'kē'	D 'dē'	E 'ē'	F 'ef'	G 'gē'	H 'hā'	I 'ī'	K 'kā'	L 'el'	M 'em'
N 'en'	O 'ō'	P 'pē'	Q 'kū'	R 'er'	S 'es'	T 'tē'	V 'ū'	X 'ix'	Y 'ypsīlon'		Z 'zēta'

30   Quid ōlim fierī velīs?

A. **Quid ōlim fierī velīs?**

B. <u>Medicus</u> fierī volō.

A. **Quam ob rem?**

B. Quia <u>hominēs adiuvāre</u> volō.

1

argentārius, nummōs numerāre

A. Quid ōlim fierī velīs?

B. _____ fierī volō.

A. Quam ob rem?

B. Quia _____ volō.

2

vigil, hominēs tuērī

A. Quid ōlim fierī velīs?

B. _____ fierī volō.

A. Quam ob rem?

B. Quia _____ volō.

3

programmātor(trix), novōs lūsūs creāre

A. _____

B. _____

A. _____

B. _____

5. Hīc scrībe sermōnem novum tuum.

A. _____

B. _____

A. _____

B. _____

4

magister (tra), discipuluōs adiuvāre

A. _____

B. _____

A. _____

B. _____

6. Hīc scrībe sermōnem alterum tuum aut sermōnem aliōrum discipulōrum.

A. Quid ōlim fierī velīs?

B. _____ fierī volō.

A. Quam ob rem?

B. Quia _____ volō.

tōns·or -trix: *barber*	māchināt·or -rix: *machinist*	fab·er -rix: *carpenter*
advocātus·us -a: *lawyer*	domised·us -a: *home maker*	ingeniāri·us -a: *engineer*
diurnāri·us -a: *journalist*	sīphōnāri·us -a: *fire fighter*	officiālis: *civil servant*
cant·or -rix: *singer*	nosocom·us -a / infirmāri·us -a / aegrōrum minist·er -ra: *nurse*	

31   Vīsne apud mē cēnāre?

    A.   **Vīsne apud <u>tabernāculum meum</u> cēnāre?**

    B.   **Mihi valdē placet. Quandō?**

    A.   <u>**Diē Sōlis.**</u>

    B.   <u>**Prīdiē Īdus Martiās?**</u>

    A.   **Sīc.**

1

A. caveam meam, Diē Veneris
B. a.d. IV Non. Īun. *

A. Vīsne apud _____ cēnāre?

B. Mihi valdē placet. Quandō?

A. _____.

B. _____?

A. Sīc.

2

A. mē, Crās
B. a.d. XIII Kal. Feb. *

A. Vīsne apud _____ cēnāre?

B. Mihi valdē placet. Quandō?

A. _____.

B. _____?

A. Sīc.

3

A. formīdulōsum castellum meum, Perendie
*B. Prīdiē Kal. Nov. ***

A. _____

B. _____

A. _____

B. _____

A. _____

5. Hīc scrībe sermōnem novum tuum.

A. _____

B. _____

A. _____

B. _____

A. _____

4

A. Īnsulam meam, Diē Lūnae
*B. a.d. III Īdūs Nov. ***

A. _____

B. _____

A. _____

B. _____

A. _____

6. Hīc scrībe sermōnem alterum tuum aut sermōnem aliōrum discipulōrum.

A. Vīsne apud _____ cēnāre?

B. Mihi valdē placet. Quandō?

A. _____.

B. _____?

A. Sīc.

* Vīde appendicem IV

32 Quam bella domus!

A.   Īntrēs, quaesō. Ōtiō<u>sus</u> estō. <u>Vīnum bibe</u>.

B.   Gratiās. Ō! Quam <u>iūcundum pōculum</u>!

A.   Suaviter dīcis. Āge ut domī suae sīs.

1

       A. ecce nucēs   *B. urbāna aedēs*

A. Īntrēs, quaesō. Ōtiōs__ estō.

   _____

B. Gratiās. Ō!

   Quam _____!

A. Suaviter dīcis. Āge ut domī suae sīs.

2

      A. Theam bibe   *B. bella domus*

A. Īntrēs, quaesō. Ōtiōs__ estō.

   _____

B. Gratiās. Ō!

   Quam _____!

A. Suaviter dīcis. Āge ut domī suae sīs.

3

A. Mūsicam ausculēmus   B. mīrificum mōnstrum

A. _____

_____

B. _____

_____

A. _____

5. Hīc scrībe sermōnem novum tuum.

A. _____

_____

B. _____

_____

A. _____

4

A. consīde in lectō   B. bellus prospectus

A. _____

_____

B. _____

_____

A. _____

6. Hīc scrībe sermōnem alterum tuum aut sermōnem aliōrum discipulōrum.

A. Īntrēs, quaeso. Ōtiōs__ estō.

_____

B. Gratiās. Ō!

Quam _____!

A. Suaviter dīcis. Āge ut domī suae sīs.

33   Quae addita sunt?

A.   **Haec cēna mihi valdē placet.**

B.   **Gratiās.**

A.   **Quid vocātur?**

B.   <u>**"Pavlova" quam māter ab Novā Zēlandiā mīsit.**</u>

A.   **Quae addita sunt?**

B.   **Em.** <u>**Albāmenta ōvōrum et saccrum**</u>

1

"Fabae Vitellianae", gingiber, piper

A. Haec cēna mihi valdē placet.

B. Gratiās.

A. Quid vocātur?

B. "_____"

A. Quae addita sunt?

B. Em. _____

2

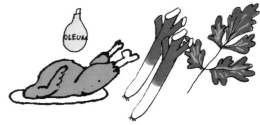

"Pullus Vardanus"
Ōleum, fasciculus porrī et coriandrum

A. Haec cēna mihi valdē placet.

B. Gratiās.

A. Quid vocātur?

B. "_____"

A. Quae addita sunt?

B. Em. _____

3

"Cucurbitae more Alexandrīnō"
sal, piper, cuminum

A. _____

B. _____

A. _____

B. _____

A. _____

B. _____

4

"Pisae Indicae"
porrum, coriandrum et sēpiās

A. _____

B. _____

A. _____

B. _____

A. _____

B. _____

5. Hīc scrībe sermōnem novum tuum.

A. _____

B. _____

A. _____

B. _____

A. _____

B. _____

6. Hīc scrībe sermōnem alterum tuum aut sermōnem aliōrum discipulōrum.

A. Haec cēna mihi valdē placet.

B. Gratiās.

A. Quid vocātur?

B. "_____"

A. Quae addita sunt?

B. Em. _____

vidē appendicem III

71

34   Scīsne?

A.   Scīsne <u>Caesarem crās interfectum īrī</u>?

B.   Verōne? Quōmodo id comperistī?

A.   <u>Augur, T. Vestricius Spurinna nōmine, mē certiōrem fēcit.</u>

B.   <u>Incrēdulus sum.</u>

1

A. fēlēs tintinnābulum gerere
Āesōpus mihi id narrāvit   *B. Laetus sum*

A.   Scīsne _____

_____?

B.   Verōne? Quōmodo id comperistī?

A.   _____.

B.   _____.

2

A. crās probātiōnem magistram nobis
impositūram esse, Amica nostra mē certiōrem
fēcit   *B. Sollicita sum*

A.   Scīsne _____

_____?

B.   Verōne? Quōmodo id comperistī?

A.   _____.

B.   _____.

3

A. aliquem cadavera ē sepulcretō abstulisse, ephēmeride   B. dē hīs admīror

A. _____

     _____

B. _____

A. _____

B. _____

4

A. procūrātōrem in aere aliēnō esse, omnēs in officīnā dē hōc colloquī   B. eius misereō

A. _____

     _____

B. _____

A. _____

B. _____

5. Hīc scrībe sermōnem novum tuum.

A. _____

     _____

B. _____

A. _____

B. _____

6. Hīc scrībe sermōnem alterum tuum aut sermōnem aliōrum discipulōrum.

A. Scīsne _____

     _____?

B. Verōne? Quōmodo id comperistī?

A. _____.

B. _____.

35   Valē!

A.   **Mihi eundum tempus est.**

B.   **Īamne abīs?**

A.   **Sīc. <u>Audīvī modo signum dārī.</u>**

B.   **Benē ambulā et redambulā.**

A.   **Quod mē invītāvistī gratiās tibi agō. Valē!**

1

tinnītum audiō

A. Mihi eundum tempus est.

B. Īamne abīs?

A. Sīc. _____.

B. Benē ambulā et redambulā.

A. Quod mē invītāvistī gratiās tibi agō. Valē!

2

Ad octāvam redīre mātrī prōmīsī

A. Mihi eundum tempus est.

B. Īamne abīs?

A. Sīc. _____.

B. Benē ambulā et redambulā.

A. Quod mē invītāvistī gratiās tibi agō. Valē!

3

somnō gravis sum

A. _____

B. _____

A. _____

B. _____

A. _____

4

caelum nocte obscūrātur

A. _____

B. _____

A. _____

B. _____

A. _____

5. Hīc scrībe sermōnem novum tuum.

A. _____

B. _____

A. _____

B. _____

A. _____

6. Hīc scrībe sermōnem alterum tuum aut sermōnem aliōrum discipulōrum.

A. Mihi eundum tempus est.

B. Īamne abīs?

A. Sīc. _____.

B. Benē ambulā et redambulā.

A. Quod mē invītāvistī gratiās tibi agō. Valē!

Latin has a very long history of being taught and learned by those who were not native speakers. Here are two examples. The first is from what is possibly the world's oldest exant foreign language textbook. A manuscript of this, about a thousand years old, is in a library at Oxford. It is called *The Colloquies of Aelfric Bata*. It was a language textbook for young monks at a Benedictine monastary learning to use Latin for their daily lives.

Colloquy 2.

Audi tu, puer, et ueni huc ad me cito, et perge ad amnem siue ad fontem, et deporta nobis [ad puteum] huc limpidam aquam cum aliquo scipho uel urceo, ut manus nostras et oculos nostros et totas facies nostras possimus lauare, quia non lauimus nos adhuc hodie.

Ibo nunc, frater, uelociter, et emendare hoc debemus.

Fac sic cito.

Veni nunc, domne me, ad me. Accipe hic modo aquam et saponem, et ita laua manus tuas et postea terge te cum lintheo nostro.

Listen, boy. Come here to me right now. Go to the stream (or spring) and bring back for us [to our cistern] here some clear water in a bowl or a pitcher so we can wash our hands, eyes and faces, since we haven't washed yet today.

I'll go right away now, brother. We should take care of that.

Do so quickly!

Come here to me now, sir. Now take this water and soap and wash your hands. Then dry yourself with our cloth.

Trans. David W. Porter. Permission to reproduce here granted by The Boydell Press.

There are many more conversations, running a wide range of human interactions; lending, lying, helping, cursing and crying. A rich and varied collection,

Below is a conversation by Martinus Corderius (Mathurin Cordier). He lived in the 1500's in France and was very active in education. John Calvin was one of his students. He wrote a large collection of conversations for students called the *Colloquiorum Scholasticorum*. These were commonly taught to students of Latin even in America from Colonial times to the late 19th century. Thomas Jefferson had a copy in his library.

A.	Visne mecum repetere praelectionem?	*Will you repeat the lesson with me?*
B.	Volo.	*I will.*
A.	Tenesne?	*Do you retain it?*
B.	Non satis recte fortasse.	*Not well enough perhaps.*
A.	Age, faciamus periculum.	*Come, let us make a trial.*
B.	Quid igitur exspectamus?	*What then do we tarry for?*
A.	Ubi voles, incipe.	*Begin when you will.*
B.	Atqui tuum est incipere.	*But it is your part to begin.*
A.	Quid ita?	*Why so?*
B.	Quia me invitasti.	*Because you have invited me.*
A.	Aequum dicis; attende igitur.	*You say right. Attend then.*
B.	Attendo, repete.	*I do attend, repeat.*

These are but two examples from the Latin education tradition. There are many more. Even a cursory look at the deep history of Latin language instruction will reveal that many modern innovations have roots in the past.

APPENDIX II   ENGLISH TRANSLATION

— 1 —

A.   Salvē! Mihi nōmen est <u>Mārcus</u>.   Hi! My name is Marcus.

B.   Ego sum <u>Maria</u>.   I'm Maria.

A.   Mihi pergrātum est tē convenīre.   I'm happy to meet you.

B.   Et mihi.   Me, too.

1: Robertus Tomus   Robert, Thomas

2: Victōria, Iohannes   Victoria, John

3: Jēms, Laura   James, Laura

4: Claudia, Hīrōkō   Claudia, Hiroko

— 2 —

A.   Salvē! Quid agis?   Hi! How are you?

B.   Bene mihi est. Quid agis tū?   Fine. How about you?

A.   Rēctē, grātiās.   Great, thanks.

     Velim trādere tibi <u>frātrem meum, Mārcum</u>.   I want to introduce you to my brother, Marcus.

B.   <u>Mārce</u>, mihi pergrātum est <u>tē</u> convenīre.   Marcus, I'm happy to meet you.

1: amīcum meum, Robertum--Roberte   My friend, Robert

2: mātrem meam, Victōriam--Victōria   My mother, Victoria

3: marītum meum, Ariovistum--Arioviste   My husband, Ariovistus

4: sorōrēs meās, Prīmam et Secūndam--Prīma et   My sisters, Prima and Secunda

   Secūnda (<u>vōs</u>)

— 3 —

A.   Quid est nōmen tibi?   What's your name?

B.   <u>Mārcus</u>.   Marcus.

A.   Unde venīs?   Where are you from?

B.   <u>Ītāliā</u>.   Italy.

A.   Ō, <u>Rōmā</u> venīs?   Oh, are you from Rome?

B.   Nōn. <u>Ostiā</u>.   No. Ostia.

1: Robertus, Americā, Atlantā--Bostōniā?   Robert, from America, Atlanta--Boston?

2: Victōria, Germāniā, Norinburgā--Berolīnō?   Victoria, from Germany, Nuremburg--Berlin?

3: Iēms, Britanniā, Cantabrigriā--Londoniō?   James, from Britain, Cambridge--London?

4: Hīrōko, Nīppōnicā, Ōsākā--Tōkyōne?   Hiroko, from Japan, Osaka--Tokyo?

— 4 —

A.   Quid est praenōmen tibi?   What's your first name?

B.   <u>Mārcus</u>.   Marcus.

A.   Quid est nōmen tibi?   What's your family name?

B.   <u>Aurēlius</u>.   Aurelius.

A.   Quot annōs nā<u>tus</u> es?   How old are you?

B.   <u>Octō et quīnquāgintā</u>.   58

1: Mohandas, Gandhi, octō et septuāgintā   Mohandas Gandhi, 78

2: Harrieta, Tubman, trēs et nōnāgintā   Harriet Tubman, 93

3: Martīnus, Luther King Jr, novem et trīgintā   Martin, Luther King Jr., 39

4: Abraham, Lincoln, sex et quīnquāgintā   Abraham Lincoln, 56

A. Salvē! Mihi nōmen est <u>Mārcus Aurēlius</u>.	Hi! My name is Marcus Aurelius.
B. Salvē! Ego sum <u>Lydia Caesar</u>.	Hi! I'm Lydia Caesar.
A. Esne cīvis <u>Americāna</u>?	Are you American?
B. Sīc. <u>Novō Eborācō</u> veniō. Et tū?	Yes. I'm from New York. And you?
A. Cīvis <u>Rōmānus</u> sum. <u>Ostiā</u> veniō.	I'm Roman. I come from Rome.

1: Maculōsus, Dalmatiānus, Spalātō-- Albus, Afghanistānus, Kabūle

Maculōsus, Dalmatia (Croatia), Spalato (Split)-- Albus, Afghan, Kabul

2: Hīrōko Ōnīshi, Nīppōnica, Ōsākā--Robertus Brown, Americānus, Geōrgiā

Hiroko Onishi, Japanese, Osaka--Robert Brown, American, Georgia

3: Mohammed al Sadat, Aegyptius, Cairōne--Anna Miller, Austrāliāna, Melburneō

Mohammed al Sadat, Egyptian, Cairo--Anna Miller, Australian, Melbourne

4: Selēna Panos, Graeca, Athenīs--Amēlia Henry, Hibernica, Dublinō

Selena Panos, Greek, Athens--Amelia Henry, Irish, Dublin

A. Salvē.	Hello.
B. Salvē! <u>Mārce</u>?	Hi! Marcus?
A. Fortasse numerum falsum habēs.	Maybe you have the wrong number.
B. Estne <u>882-6780</u>?	Is this 882-6780?
A. Nōn.	No.
B. Ō. Ignōsce mihi.	O, sorry.

1: Roberte?, 343-5129   Robert?, 343-5129

2: Claudia?, 687-4632   Claudia?, 687-4632

3: Laura?, 501-2833   Laura?, 501-2833

4: Mohammed?, 772-9460   Mohammed?, 772-9460

A. Salvē.	Hi.
B. Salvē! Adestne <u>Mārcus</u> illīc?	Hi! Is Marcus there?
A. Nōn adest. Nunc <u>in lūdō</u> est.	No he isn't. He's at school now.
B. Intellegō. Iterum tēlephōnābō.	I see. I'll call again.
A. Valē.	Good bye.

1: Robertus? in argentāriā   Robert? in the bank

2: Claudia? in tabernā vestiāriā   Claudia? at the clothing shop

3: Mohammed? in stadiō   Mohammed? at the stadium

4: Laura? in pīstrīnā   Laura? at the bakery

A. Mārce? Quid agis?	Marcus? How are you?
B. Bene, sed nunc occupā<u>tus</u> sum. <u>Cubiculum purgō</u>.	Fine, but I'm busy. I'm cleaning my room.
A. Ō. Ignōsce mihi.	Oh, sorry.
B. Nōlī sollicitārī. Posteā tē tēlephōnicē vocābō.	Don't worry. I'll call you later.
A. Bene. Valeās.	OK. Good bye.

1: Julī, Bellum gerō   Caesar, waging war

2: Phaëthon, Sōlem per aerēs trahō   Phaeton, pulling the sun

3: Tullī, Rem pūblicam servō   Cicero, saving the republic

4: Apollō, Puellam petō   Apollo, chasing a girl

— 9 —

A. Quota hōra est?
B. <u>Quārta</u> hōra.
A. Ō! Mihi eundum est.
    Opus est mihi <u>litterās dāre</u>.
B. Bene. Iterum conveniāmus.
1: tertia, domum redīre
2: tertia et dīmidia, librum bibliothēcae reddere
3: sexta, pānem emere
4: quarta et dīmidia, cēnam coquere

What time is it?
It's four.
Oh. I've got to go.
    I have to go home.
OK. Let's meet again.
3, mail a letter
3:30, take a book to the library
6, buy some bread
4:30, cook dinner

— 10 —

A. Quotā hōrā <u>bellum Germānicum</u> incipiet?
B. <u>Secundā</u> hōrā.
A. Quid! Tantum <u>quīnque</u> minūtae remanent.
B. Nōbīs festīnandum est!
1: pellicula, tertiā, decem
2: cēna apud Catullum, quīntā, vīgintī
3: Circus, Hodiē māne nōnā, quīnque et vīgintī
4: Ōrātio Cicerōnis, prīmā et dīmidiā, quīndecim

What time will the German War begin?
At two.
What! We only have five minutes.
We have to hurry!
the movie, 3, ten minutes
dinner at Catullus' house, 5, 20 minutes
Circus, 9 am, 25 minutes
Cicero's speech, 1:30, 15 minutes

— 11 —

A. Ad macellum eō ut <u>māla</u> emam.
    Possumne tibi aliquid emere?
B. Etiam. <u>Pira</u> emās, quaesō.
A. <u>Quot</u>?
B. <u>Duo aut tria</u> satis putō.
1: vīnum, fabās cafēae, Quantum, duo aut tria chilio-
    grammata.
2: oleum, lāc, Quantum, ūnam aut duās ampullās
3: piscēs, pānēs, Quot, quattuor aut quīnque
4: carnem, sanguinem, Quantum, trēs aut quattuor am-
    pullās

I'm going to the store to buy apples.
    Can I get you something?
Yes. Please buy some pears.
How many?
2 or 3 will do.
wine, coffee, How much, 2 or 3 kilograms

oil, juice, How much, 1 or 2 bottles
fish, bread, How much, 4 or 5 loaves
meat, blood, How much, 3 or 4 jars

— 12 —

A. Salvē! Quid agis?
B. Bellē. Et tū?
A. Mē bene habeō. Quō īs?
B. <u>Ad stadium</u>. Et tū?
A. <u>Ad forum</u>. Numquid vīs?
B. Ut valeās.
1: ad tōnstrīnam, Domum
2: ad theātrum, ad librāriam
3: ad tabernam flōrālem, ad gymnasium
4: ad thermās, ad lūdum

Hi! How are you?
Good. And you?
I'm fine. Where are you going?
To the stadium. And you?
To the mall. Anything else?
Just take care.
to the barber, home
to the theater, to the bookshop
to the flower shop, to the gym
to the baths, to school

13

A. Licetne mihi aliquid rogāre?   May I ask a question?
B. Quippe.   Sure.
A. Licetne mihi lūdere?   May I play?
B. Licet/ Nōn licet.   Yes/ no.

1: crās pēnsum trādere   hand in my homework tomorrow
2: scrīptūram meam per litterās ēlectronicās dāre   send my report by email
3: graphidem cuspidāre   sharpen my pencil
4: tēlevīsiōnem spectāre   watch TV

A. Ignōsce mihi. Ubi est argentāria?   Excuse me. Where's the bank?
B. Argentāria? Est iūxtā pīstrīnam.   The bank? It's next to the bakery.
A. Iūxtā pīstrīnam?   Next to the bakery?
B. Itast.   That's right.
A. Grātiās.   Thanks.
B. Libenter.   You're welcome.

1: pīstrīna, exadversum bibliothēcam   Bakery, across from the library
2: bibliothēca, inter aedem cursuālem et dēversōrium   Library, between the post office & the hotel
3: aedes cursuālis, exadversum popīnam   Post office, across from the restaurant
4: popīna, inter pīstrīnam et valētūdinārium   Restaurant, between the bakery & the hospital

15

A. Vīdistīne galeam meam?   Have you seen my hat?
B. Estne haec tua?   It this yours?
A. Nōn. Ista est antīqua. Mea est nova.   No. That is old. Mine is new.
B. Ō. Galea tua est in medianō.   Oh. Your hat is in the living room

1: canem meum, magnus, parvus-- in hortō   my dog, big, small-- in the garden
2: librum meum, Mathēmaticus, Latīnus--in locō sēcrētō.   my book, Math, Latin--in the restroom
3: fīlium meum, probus, improbus, in cubiculō magistrī summī   my son--good, bad-- in the principal's office
4: caput meum, simile mōnstrō, simile pepōnī, sub ponte   my head, like a monster, like a pumpkin--under the bridge.

16

A. Salvē, domine (domina). Possumne tibi ministrāre?   Hello, sir (ma'am). Can I help you?
B. Potes. Opus est mihi togā.   Yes. I need a toga.
A. Togae sunt illīc.   Togas are over there.
B. Grātiās.   Thank you.

1: stolā, stolae   a dress, dresses
2: brācīs, brācae   pants, pants
3: cingulō, cingula   a belt, belts
4: lūsū computātrālī, lūsūs computātrālēs   a computer game, computer games

— 17 —

A. Quantī <u>illa toga</u> cōnsta<u>t</u>?
How much is that toga?

B. <u>Haec toga vīgintī dollarīs cōnstat.</u>
This toga is twenty dollars.

A. Ostende mihi <u>illam</u>.
Show it to me.

B. Ecce.
Here.

A. Satis. Emam.
OK. I'll take it.

1: illa stola, Haec stola quīnquāgintā dollarīs cōnstat, illam
that dress, This dress costs $50.

2: illae brācae, Hae brācae sexāgintā dollarīs cōnstant, illās
those pants, These pants cost $60.

3: illud cingulum, Hoc cingulum quīnque et trīgintā dollarīs cōnstat, illud
that belt, This belt costs $35.

4: ille lūsus computātrālis, Hic lūsus duodēvīgintī dollarīs cōnstat, illum
that computer game, This game costs $18.

— 18 —

A. Vide! <u>Novam autoraedam</u> habeō. Quid cēnsēs?
I have a new car. What do you think?

B. Babae! <u>Ista est optima.</u>
Wow. It's great.

A. Grātiās. Laetissimus sum.
Thanks. I'm very happy.

1: Novam stolam, Ista est pulchra.
A new dress, That's beautiful.

2: Novās brācās, Istae sunt iūcundae.
New pants, They're nice.

3: Novum cingulum, Istud est bellum.
A new belt, That's pretty.

4: Novum lūsum computātrālem, Iste est mīrificus.
A new computer game, That's fantastic.

— 19 —

A. <u>Calētur</u> hodiē. Vīsne <u>natāre in lacū</u>?
It's hot today. Do you want to swim in the lake?

B. Bonum cōnsilium! <u>Natēmus.</u>
Good idea! Let's swim.

1: Ningit, forīs lūdere, lūdāmus
snowing, play outside

2: Pluit, pelliculam spectāre, spectēmus
raining, see a movie

3: Sūdum est, per hortōs dēambulāre, dēambulēmus
nice, walk in the park

4: Ventōsum est, nāvigāre, nāvigēmus
windy, go sailing

— 20 —

A. Aliquid ūnā agēmus hodiē?
Shall we do something together today?

B. Bene. <u>In lacū natēmus.</u>
OK. Let's swim in the lake.

A. Em. abhinc hebdomadem unam <u>in lacū natāvimus</u>. Vīsne <u>currere per hortōs</u>?
Well, we swam in the lake last week. Do you want to run in the park?

B. Bene. <u>Currāmus.</u>
OK. Let's run.

1: forīs lūdāmus, forīs lūsimus, ad forum īre, eāmus
play outside, played outside, go to the mall, let's go

2: pelliculam spectēmus, pelliculam spectāvimus, pilā lūdere, Pilā lūdāmus.
see a movie, saw a movie, play ball, let's play ball

3: per hortōs dēambulēmus, dēambulāvimus, saltāre, Saltēmus
walk through the park, took a walk, dance, let's dance

4: nāvigēmus, nāvigāvimus, piscātum īre, Eāmus
go sailing, went sailing, go fishing, let's go

— 21 —

A. Hāc nocte tēlephōnicē vocāvī, sed abfuistī.
B. Etiam. <u>In theātrō</u> eram.
A. Quid cēnsuistī?
B. <u>Bonum erat.</u>

1: In forō cum amīcīs, iūcundum erat.
2: In carcere, Malum erat.
3: In cūriā, Clāmōsa erat.
4: In amphitheātrō, Ah, etiamnunc vīvō.

I called you last night but you weren't home.
Yes. I was at the theater.
How was it? (what did you think?)
Nice.

at the mall with my friends, It was fun.
in jail, It was bad.
in the Senate, It was noisy.
in the amphitheater. Well, I'm still alive.

— 22 —

A. Quid agēs crās?
B. <u>Ad forum emptum ībō.</u> Et tū?
A. <u>Ad merīdiem dormiam.</u>

1: Cum amīcō lūdam, Cubiculum purgābō
2: Ad lītus ībō, Aliquās litterās ēlectronicās amīcīs dābō.
3: Pedifolle lūdam, Notās meās prō probātiōne ēdiscam
4: Aviam vīsitābō, Birotam resarciam

What will you do tomorrow?
I'll go shopping in the mall. And you?
I will sleep until noon.

I will play with my friend, I'll clean my room.
I'll go to the beach, I'll send some emails to my friends.
I'll play football, I'll study my notes for the test.

I'll visit my grandmother, I'll fix my bike.

— 23 —

A. Quid herī ēgistī?
B. <u>Ad forum emptum īvī.</u>
A. Bonum vidētur.
B. Bonum erat. Et tū?
A. <u>Ad merīdiem dormīvī.</u>

1: Cum amīcō lūsī, Cubiculum purgāvī.
2: Ad lītus īvī, Aliquās litterās ēlectronicās amīcīs dēdī.
3: Pedifolle lūsī, Notās meās prō probātiōne ēdidicī.
4: Aviam vīsitāvī, Birotam resarsī

What did you do yesterday?
I went shopping in the mall.
That seems nice.
It was. And you?
I slept until noon.

I played with a friend, I cleaned my room.
I went to the beach, I sent some emails to my friends.
I played football, I studied my notes for the test.
I visited my grandmother, I fixed my bike.

— 24 —

A. Nōn salv<u>us</u> sum.
B. Quid est tibi?
A. <u>Caput mihi dolet.</u>
B. Cūrā ut valeās.

1: Stomachus mihi dolet.
2: Tussiō.
3: Febriō.
4: Gravēdine labōrō.

I don't feel well.
What's wrong?
I have a headache.
Take care.

I have a stomachache.
I have a cough.
I have a fever.
I have a cold.

82

— 25 —

A. Tū īrāta vidēris.
B. Plānē. Īrāta sum.
A. Quam ob rem?
B. Quod discipulī meī pēnsa nōn cōnficiunt!

1: laetus, crās erit diēs Sāturnī
2: tristis, canis meus est mortuus
3: sollicitus, crās erit probātiō Latīna
4: timidus, iamiamque post tē umbram vīdī

You seem angry.
Yes. I'm angry.
Why?
Because my students don't do their assignments.

Happy, tomorrow will be Saturday
Sad, my dog died.
Worried, there will be a Latin test tomorrow
Afraid, I just saw a ghost behind you.

— 26 —

A. Māvīsne māla an pira?
B. Māla mālō. Et tū?
A. Ego pira.

1: fēlēs an canēs
2: aestātem an hiemem
3: librōs legere an litterās scrībere
4: mūsicam audīre an pelliculam spectāre

Which do you like better, apples or pears?
I like apples better. How about you?
I prefer pears.

cats or dogs
summer or winter
reading books or writing letters
listening to music or watching a movie

— 27 —

A. Quid tē hodiē dēlectet?
B. Isicium Hamburgense et solāna frīcta (velim).
A. Aliquam pōtiōnem?
B. Coca-cōlam.
A. Edāsne hīc an forīs?
B. Forīs / Hīc.

1: rēticulatās et farcīmina, cafēam
2: collȳrās et acētāria, theam
3: būbulam assam, lāc
4: ōva frīcta et lardum, aurantiī pōtiōnem

What would you like today?
(I'll have) a burger and fries.
Anything to drink?
A coke.
Is that for here or to go?
To go /Here.

waffles and sausages, coffee
pasta and salad, tea
roast beef, milk
fried eggs and bacon, orange juice

— 28 —

A. Illīc est domus mea.
B. Quaenam?
A. Illa est albā iānuā.
B. Et duābus fenestrīs?
A. Sīc.
1: māter mea, Quaenam, Illa est caeruleō petasō, longā
   stolā
2: computātrum meum, Quodnam, Illud est iūxtā
   antīquum impressōrium, infractō monitōriō
3: liber meus, Quisnam, Ille est iūcundīs pictūrīs,
   mōnstruōsīs sermōnibus
4: homō, Quisnam, Ille est oculīs duōbus, ūnō nāsō

That's my house over there.
Which one?
The one with the white door.
And two windows?
Yes.
my mother, Which, The one with the blue hat, long
   dress
my computer, Which, The one next to the old printer,
   broken monitor
my book, Which, the one with the funny pictures,
   strange dialogues
a human, Who, the one with two eyes, one nose

29

A.   Ūterisne interrēte?
B.   Ūtor. Cūr?
A.   Dā mihi, sōdēs, litterās ēlectronicās dē <u>hodiernō</u>
     <u>pēnsō</u>.
B.   Libenter. Quam inscriptiōnem ēlectronicam habēs?
A.   Mea est <u>marcus@SPQR.gov</u>.
1: crastinā probātiōne, maria@studēbō.com
2: pugnā cum barbarīs, metuēns@fugiō.com
3: quō manipulō lūsum vicerit, egoeō@nōnvideō.com
4: quōmodo haec cēna parātur,
     novissimus@coquus.com

Are you on line?
Yes, why?
Can you send me an email about today's homework?

No problem. What's your email address?
It's marcus@SPQR.gov
tomorrow's test, maria@studebo.com
the battle with the barbarians, metuens@fugio.com
who wins the game, egoeo@nonvideo.com
how to make this dinner, novissimus@coquus.com

30

A.   Quid ōlim fierī velīs?
B.   <u>Medicus</u> fierī volō
A.   Quam ob rem?
B.   Quia <u>hominēs adiuvāre</u> volō.
1: argentārius, nummōs numerāre
2: vigil, hominēs tuērī
3: programmātor(trix), novōs lūsūs creāre
4: magister(tra), discipulōs adiuvāre

What do you want to be in the future?
I'd like to be a doctor.
Why?
Because I want to help people.
banker, count money
police officer, protect people
computer programmer, make new games
teacher, help students

31

A.   Vīsne apud tabernāculum meum cēnāre.
B.   Mihi valdē placet. Quandō?
A.   <u>Diē Sōlis.</u>
B.   <u>Prīdiē Īdus Martiās?</u>
A.   Sīc.
1. caveam meam, Diē Veneris, ante diem quartam
     Nōnās Īuniās
2. mē, Crās, ante diem tertiam decimam Kalendās Feb-
     ruariās
3. formīdulōsum castellum meum, Perendiē, Prīdiē
     Kalendās Novembrēs
4. īnsulam meam, Diē Lūnae, ante diem tertiam Īdūs
     Novembrēs

Would you like to dine at my place?
I'd love to. When?
On Sunday.
On March 14th?
Yes.
1. my hole, on Friday, February 2nd

2. my tent, Tomorrow, January 20th.

3. my scary castle, the day after tomorrow, October
     31st.

4. my apartment, on Monday, November 11th.

32

A.   Intrēs, quaeso. Ōtiō<u>sus</u> estō. <u>Vīnum bibe</u>.
B.   Gratiās. Ō! Quam <u>iūcundum pōculum</u>!
A.   Suaviter dīcis. Āge ut domī suae sīs.

1. Ecce nucēs, urbāna aedēs
2. Theam bibe, bella domus
3. Mūsicam ausculēmus, mīrificum mōnstrum
4. Cōnsīde in lectō, bellus prospectus

Come in please. Relax. Drink some wine.
Thanks. Oh, what a nice cup.
You say the nicest things. Make yourself at home.

1. here are some nuts, classy house.
2. drink some tea, a lovely house.
3. let's listen to some music, great monster.
4. sit on the sofa, nice view.

— 33 —

A. Haec cēna mihi valdē placet.	This dinner is great.
B. Gratiās.	Thanks.
A. Quid vocātur?	What's it called?
B. "Pavlova" quam māter ab Novā Zēlandiā mīsit.	"Pavlova" which my mother sent from New Zealand
A. Quae addita sunt?	What's in it?
B. Ēm. Albāmenta ōvōrum et saccrum.	Well, egg white and sugar.

1. "Fabae Vitellianae", gingiber, piper
2. "Pullus Vardanus", Ōelum, fasciculus porrī et coriandrum.
3. "Cucurbitae more Alexandrīnō", sal, piper, cuminum
4. "Pisae Indicae", porrum, coriandrum et sēpiās

1. "Beans à la Vitellio", ginger and pepper
2. "Vardan chicken", oil, a bunch of leeks and coriander.
3. "Pumpkin, Alexandrine Style", salt, pepper, cumin
4. "Indian Peas", leeks, coriander and squid.

— 34 —

A. Scīsne Caesarem crās interfectum īrī.	Do you know that Caesar will be killed tomorrow?
B. Verōne? Quōmodo id comperistī?	Really? How did you find that out?
A. Āugur, T. Vestricius Spurinna nōmine, mē certiōrem fēcit.	An augur named Titus Vestricius Spurinna informed me.
B. Incrēdulus sum.	I'm incredulous.

1. fēlēs tintinnābulum gerere, Āesōpus mihi id narrāvit, Laetus sum

2. crās probātiōnem magistram nobis impositūram esse, Amica nostra mē certiōrem fēcit, Sollicita sum

3. aliquem cadavera ē sepulcretō abstulisse, ephēmeride, dē hīs admīror

4. procūrātōrem in aere aliēnō esse, omnēs in officīnā dē hōc colloquī, eius misereo

1. The cat has a bell. Aesop told me, I'm happy.

2. Our teacher will give us a test tomorrow, Our friend informed me, I'm upset.

3. someone has stolen bodies from the cemetery, the paper, I'm shocked.
4. the boss is in debt, everyone in the office is talking about it, I feel sad for him

— 35 —

A. Mihi eundum tempus est.	It's time for me to go.
B. Īamne abīs?	Leaving already?
A. Sīc. Audīvī modo signum dārī.	Yes. I've just heard the signal given.
B. Benē ambulā et redambulā.	Walk safely and come again!
A. Quod mē invītāvistī gratiās tibi agō. Valē!	Thanks for inviting me. Good bye!

1. tinnītum audiō,
2. Ad octāvam redīre mātrī prōmīsī.
3. somnō gravis sum.
4. caelum obscūrātur.

1. I hear a ringing.
2. I promised my mom I'd be home by 8.
3. I'm sleepy.
4. It's getting dark.

APPENDIX III   WORDS AND PHRASES

• Activities •

feed the dog / cat / mouse	canī / fēlī / mūrī cibum dāre	- paper	chartulae ineptae
walk the dog	canem ducere	sweep the floor (with a broom)	pavīmentum verrere (scopā)
wash clothes, laundry	lavandaria ēluere	to form a conspiracy	coniūrātiōnem facere
wash dishes	patinās lavāre	to form a plan.	consillium capēre
to change one's clothes	vestīmenta (et calceōs) mūtāre	to shake hands	dextram iungere cum aliquō; dextrās inter sē iungere
comb hair	capillōs pectere		
brush teeth	dentēs pergāre	to buy dearly	magnō / malē emere
make a bed	lectulum sternō, sternere, strāvī, strātus	to buy cheaply	parvō / vīlī pretiō / benē emere
get up	surgere	to be free from business	negōtiīs vacāre
go shopping	obsōnāre	to go to meet someone	obviam venīre alicui
go to bed	cubitum īre	to award a prize to someone	pālmam deferre (dāre) alicui
set the table	mēnsam pōnere		
water the flowers	flōrēs irrigāre	to offer a prize/reward	praemium expōnere (prōpōnere)
to take out	aufero, auferre, abstuli, ablātum	to journey together	ūnā iter facere
garbage	quisquiliae -ārum f pl; purgāmentum ī		

• Animals •

ant	formīca, ae	duck	anas, -atis f
ape	sīmius, -ī; sīmia ae	eagle	aquila, -ae f
bat	vespertiliō, -ōnis m	elephant	elephantus, -ī m
bear	ursus, -ī; ursa, -ae	fish	piscis, -is m
bee	apis, -is f	fly	musca, -ae f
bird	avis, -is f	fox	vulpēs, -is f
boar	aper, -rī m	frog	rāna, -ae f
camel	camēlus, -ī m	goat	caper, -rī m; capra, -ae f
cat	fēlis (fēlēs), -is f	goose	anser, -eris m
chicken	pullus, -ī m	hen	gallīna, -ae f
cockroach	blatta -ae f	horse	equus, -ī mf
cow	vacca, -ae	insect	īnsectum, ī n
crocidile	crocodīlus, ī m	lamb	agnus, -ī m
crow	cornīx, -īcis f	lion	leō, -ōnis m; leana, -ae f
deer	cervus, -ī m; cerva, -ae f	monkey	(see ape)
dog	canis, -is mf	mouse	mūs, -ris m
donkey	asinus, -ī m	owl	būbō, -ōnis m

ox	bōs, bovis m	sheep	ovis, -is f
pet	dēliciae, -ārum fpl	snake	anguis, -is mf
pig	porcus, -ī m	sow	sūs, is f
pigeon	columbus, -ī m; columba, -ae f	sparrow	passer, -eris m
		spider	arāneus, -ī m
pup	catulus, -ī m	tiger	tigris, -is (or -idis) m
rabbit	cunīculus, -ī m	wasp	vespa, -ae f
ram	ariēs, -etis m	whale	balaena, -ae f
rat	(see *mouse*)	wolf	lupus, -ī m; lupa, -ae f
raven	corvus, -ī m	worm	vermis, -is m
rooster	gallus, -ī m		
serpent	serpēns, -entis m		

• Colors •

black	āter, -tra, -trum	orange	aurantius, -a, -um
blond	flāvus, -a, -um	pink	subroseus, -a, -um
blue	cyaneus, -a, -um	purple	purpureus, -a, -um
sky-blue	caeruleus, -a, -um	red	rūfus, -a, -um; ruber, -bra, -brum
brown	fulvus, -a, -um		
golden	aureolus, -a, -um	silvery	argenteus, -a, -um
gray	cinereus, -a, -um	white	albus, -a, -um
green	viridis, -is, -e	yellow	flāvus, -a, -um
lavender	caesius, -a, -um		

• Conversation Gambits •

As far as I know.	quod sciam; quoad sciō, quantum sciō	That depends.	Ex rē pendet.
		to be frank	ut vērum confitear
by the way, incidentally	ceterum; ut hoc obiter addam / dīcam; in trānsitū attingo	Unless I'm mistaken.	nisi fallor; nisi mē fallit
		allow me to say	pāce tuā dixerim; dīcere liceat
Enough said.	sat superque (dē illā rē); haec hactenus; plura dīcere supersedēbō	I want a word with you.	paucīs (tribus verbis) tē volō.
I agree with you.	Tibi assentiō (assentior)	to make mention of	mentiōnem facere alicuius reī (dē aliquā rē)
I'd like to ask you	Velim ē tē sciscitāri		
I'm not sure.	Haud mihi explōrātum est; Nōn certus sum	to pass on to other things	ad reliqua pergāmus
		to change topics	sermōnem aliō trasfere
in my opinion,	meā (quidem) sententiā; meā opīnione, secundum mē; ex meō arbitriō	as Cicero says	ut ait Cicerō
		Everyone says.	vulgō dicitur.

• Fighting Words •

Go to the Devil!	Ī in malam rem!	*What are you mad about?*	Quid tibi stomachō est?
	Abī in malam crucem!	*Who gave you that name?*	Quis hoc tibi nōmen imposuit?
Come on!	Age!		
May the gods curse you!	Dī tē perdant!	*What happened then?*	Quid tum posteā?
Block head!	Caudex!	*He pushed me.*	Extrūsit mē dē locō.
Crook!	Sceleste!	*He punched me.*	Pugnōs mihi impēgit.
Liar!	Mendax; Periūre!	*He tripped up my heels.*	Mē supplantāvit.
You're crazy!	Dēlīrās!	*You make me angry.*	Mihi aegrē facis.
You're joking.	Garrīs!	*Mind your own business.*	Tuās rēs perage.
Shut up!	Opprime ōs!	*It's none of my business.*	Rēs mē nihil contingit.
Do not cry.	Ōmitte lacrimās.	*You touch a sore spot.*	Tangis ulcus.
Why this dispute?	Quorsus haec disputātio?	*I blame this in you.*	Hoc in tē reprehendō.
What have I done?	Quid offendi?	*unable to hold back tears*	lacrimās tenēre nōn posse
How have I done wrong?	Quā in rē peccāvī?		

• Food •

There is an ancient cookbook here: http://www.thelatinlibrary.com/apicius.html
An English translation is here: http://penelope.uchicago.edu/Thayer/E/Roman/Texts/Apicius/1*.html

meat	carnō, nis f	*sour*	acidus, -a -um
fish	piscātus, ūs, m	*salty*	salsus, -a -um
chicken	gallīnācea, ae	*sandwich*	pastillum (-ī n) fartum
pork	porcīna, ae	*delicious*	dēlectābilīs, dēlectābile; dēliciōsus,-a -um
beef	būbula, ae		
egg	ōvum, ī n		
milk	lāc, lactis, n	***vegetables***	**(h)olera (npl.)**
cheese	cāseus, ī m	*vegetarian*	frugivorus, a; sōlīs holeribus et farīnāceīs vescēns
flour	farīna, ae		
bread	pānis, is m		
toast	pānis tostus	*artichoke*	cinara, ae
salt	sāl, salis n	*asparagus*	asparagus, ī
water	aqua, ae f	*bean*	faba, ae
wine	vīnum, ī n	*beet*	bēta, ae
milk	lāc, lactis n	*broccoli*	brassica (-ae, f.) ītalica
vinegar	acētum, ī n	*Brussels sprouts*	brassica gemmifera
breakfast	ientāculum, ī n	*cabbage*	brassica, ae
lunch	prandium, ī n	*sauerkraut*	brassica condīta
dinner	cēna, ae f	*carrot*	carōta, ae
sweet	dulcis, dulce	*cauliflower*	(brassica) cauliflora, ae
		chickpea	cicer, eris, n.

coleslaw	acētāria brassicae
corn / maize	mays, maydis f.
corn cob	spīca maydis
cucumber	cucumis, eris m.
eggplant	melongena, ae
French fries	terrestria pōma fricta npl.; solāna fricta
garlic	ālium, ī
gourd	cucurbita, ae
grape	ūva, ae
green bean	phaseolus, ī
leek	porrum, ī
lentil	lēns, tis f.
lettuce	lactūca, ae
head of lettuce	lactūcae cap•ut, -itis, n.
mushroom	bōlētus, ī
toadstool	fung(ul)us, ī
mustard	sināpis, is f.
onion	caepa, ae
parsnip	pastinaca, ae
peanut	arachis, idis f.
pepper (green or red)	capsicum, ī
pepper (spice)	piper, eris n.
pimento	pimenta, ae
popcorn	maīzium inflātum n.
potato	pōmum terrestre n.
mashed potatoes	pōmōrum terrestrium puls, -tis f.
potato chips	lāminae solānōrum fpl.
radish	raphanus, ī
rhubarb	radix Pontica; reubarbum
salad	acētāria, ōrum npl.
tossed	lactūca ex acētō et sāle sparsa
soup	iūs, iūris, n.
spinach	spinacium, ī
squash	cucurbita, ae
sweet potato	batāta, ae
tomato	lycopersicum, ī; tomāta, ae
tomato sauce	lycopersicī liquāmen, inis n.
turnip	rāpum, ī
fruit	**pōma, -ōrum (npl.)**
apple	mālum, ī
- pie	scriblīta ex mālīs facta
-sauce	puls (pultis, f) mālōrum
apricot	Prūnum armeniacum: armeniacum (pomum)
avocado	Persea americāna
banana	ariēna, ae
berry	baca, ae
blackberry	mōrum, ī
blueberry	myrtī mōrum, ī
currant	ribēsium, ī
raspberry	rubum īdaeum
strawberry	frāga (n. pl.)
cherry	cerasum, ī
grapefruit	(citrum) paradisiacum; citrum grande
lemon	Citrus limonum:
-peel	cortex (-ticis, m.) citrī
lemonade	pōsca citronāta; limonāta; pōtio (-ōnis f.) citrea; limonāta
lime	limon, ōnis f.; citreum viride
mandarin orange	mandarīnum, ī
orange	mālum Sinicum; mālum Sinense; mālum aureum
date	palm(ul)a, ae
fruit juice	sucus (-ī m.) fructuārius; sucus pōmōrum
grape juice	sucus ūvae; ūmor Bacchī [Virg.]
kiwi	grussularia Sinensis; kivium, ī
mango	mangus, ī
melon	melō, ōnis m.; melō, melōpepo, -ōnis, m.

cantaloupe	Cucumis melō: melō	*chive*	c(a)epa, ae
peach	mālum Persicum	*chives*	porrum sectile
pineapple	mālum pīneum	*cinnamon*	cinnamōmum, ī
plum	Prūnus domesticus	*clove*	garyophyll·on, ī n.
pomegranate	(mālum) Pūnicum	*curry*	iūs (iūris, n) condīmentī indicī
watermelon	melō (-ōnis m.) aquōsus		
		ginger	gingiber, gingiberis n.
nut	**nux, nucis f.**	*lavender*	lavendula, ae
almond	amygdala, ae	*licorice*	glycyrrhiz·on,ī n.; dulcis rādix, īxis, f.
cashew	anacardus, ī		
chestnut	castanea, ae	*mace*	macis, idis f.
-roasted	castanea tosta	*menthol*	methōlum, ī
coconut	nux Indica magna; nux cocoīna ; cocus	*mustard*	sināpis, is f.
		nutmeg	(nux) musata, ae
-milk	latex (-ticis, m.) ex nuce cocō	*paprika*	piperatum Hungaricum, ī
		parsley	petroselinum; apium, ī
peanut	arachis, idis f.	*pepper (spice)*	piper, eris n.
pistachio	pistacium, ī	*peppermint*	mentha (ae f.) piperītidis; mentha piperīta
walnut	iūglāns, antis f.		
		rosemary	rosmarīnus, ī
spice	**condīmentum, ī**	*sesame*	sesamum, sesama; (seed) sēmen (-minis, n) sesamae
(sprinkle)	aspergo, conspergo		
spicy	condītus, a, um		
basil	ōcimum, ī	*thyme*	thymum, ī
camomille	chamaemēl·on, ī n.	*vanilla*	vanilla, ae
caraway	careum, ī		
- seed	careī sēmina, ōrum npl.		

• Health •

I am sick.	Aeger, -ra sum.	*I never felt better.*	Sic valeō ut nunquam melius.
I have a cold	Gravēdine labōrō		
What is your ailment?	Quis tē morbus habet?	*How is is your brother?*	Quid frāter?
What's bothering you?	Quae rēs tē agitat?	*Is he well?*	salvus est?
How did you get that?	Unde istum morbum contraxistī?	*Is everyone well at home?*	Rectēne apud vōs?
		His sickness worsens.	Ingravēscit morbus.
I am well.	Bene mihi est.	*I have a cough.*	Tussiō.
I am a little better.	Melius (meliuscule) mihi est.	*I have a fever.*	Febriō.
		I have indigestion.	Crūdō stomachō labōrō.
I am not yet well.	Nōn plānē ā morbō convaluī.	*I have diarrhea.*	dēiectiōne labōrō.
		He has a nose bleed.	Sanguis eī nāribus mānat, fluit.
I am not very well.	Minus bellē mē habēs.		

	Nāribus sanguinem ēmittit.	*to refresh oneself with food, wine, sleep*	corpus cūrāre (cibō, vīnō, somnō)
He has sore eyes.	Labōrat ex oculīs.	*to be hungry*	ēsurīre
I am seriously ill.	In malīs aeger sum.	*to be starving*	fame labōrāre (premī)
I have no desire to vomit.	Nausea plānē abiit.	*to slake one's thirst with a draught of cold water*	
bless you (for a sneeze)	Sit faustum ac felix		sitim haustū gelidae aquae sēdāre
take care of yourself	Valētūdinem tuam cūrā diligenter		

• Opinion •

What is your opinion?	Quid sentis?	*I'll think about it.*	Dē hōc valdē viderō.
Are you of this opinion?	Siccine est sententia?	*I do not doubt it.*	Id nōn dubito.
What advice do give me?	Quid mihi auctor es? Quid mihi suādēs?	*Without any doubt.*	Absque dubiō. Sine dubiō.
In my opinion.	Meā (quidem) sententiā	*You are right.*	Est ita, ut dīcis. Rectē dīcis. Vērum est.
We have the same opinion.	Nostrī sensūs congruunt.	*You're wrong.*	Errās.
I am of your opinion.	Tibi assentiō, tēcum sentiō, tuae sententiae faveō.	*Believe me.*	Mihi crede.

• Places •

house	domus, -us, f.	*residence hall*	contubernium, -ī, n
yard	area, -ae, f.	*room-mate*	contubernālis, -is, c
kitchen	culīna, -ae, f.	*countryside*	rūs, rūris, n.
bedroom	cubiculum, ī, n.	*city*	urbs, urbis, f.
room	conclāve, -is, n.	*United States of America*	Cīvitātēs Foederātae Americae (Septentriōnālis)
neighborhood	vicus, -ī, m..		
library	bibliothēca, -ae, f.	*South America*	America Merīdiāna
lounge	conclāve remissivum		
office	locus officiālis		

• Requests •

Please	sōdēs (sī audēs)	*to permit, grant*	Dare cōpiam, facultātem, potestātem, licentiam.
[informal]	vīn' (vīsne) amābō, amābō tē sīs (sī vīs) sultis (sī vultis)	*Permit me, I pray you,*	Date mihi, quaesō, veniam ut...
[formal]	orō quaesō obsecrō	*I permit you to go.*	Per mē ut abeās licet.
		I will permit you that.	Tibi permissūrus sum ut hoc faciās.
Does that suit you?	Placetne tibi?	*He has never refused me.*	Nihil unquam mihi abnuit.

You refuse such a little thing.	Mihi dēnegās quod tantī nōn est.	*I am at your service.*	Tōtus tuus sum.
Do me this favor.	Adhibe ergā mē istud beneficium.	*I shall never forget it.*	Numquam illīus memoria effluet.
Nothing will I do more willingly.	Nihil est aeque quod faciam lubēns.	*I'm much obliged.*	Benignē dīcis.
		It s very kind of you.	Benignē fēcistī.
		Don't mention it.	nōn est cūr (mihi grātiās) agās.

• School •

school	lūdus, -ī, m.	locker	capsa, -ae, f.
room	conclāve, -is, n	lesson	lectiō, -ōnis, f.
interior wall	pariēs, -etis, f.	homework	pēnsum, -ī, n.
blackboard	tabula, -ae, f.	*Open*	Aperī, Aperīte
window	fenestra, -ae, f.	*Close*	Claude, Claudite
door	iānua, -ae, f.	*Be quiet!*	Tacē, Tacēte
piece of paper	folium, -iī, n.	*Listen*	Auscultā, Auscultāte
page	pāgina, -ae, f.	*Recite*	Recitā, Recitāte
notebook	libellus, -ī, m.	*Read (silently)*	Lege, legite
chalk	crēta, -ae, f.	to give a test	probātiōnem impōnere
pen	stīlus, -ī, m.	to take a test	probātiōnem subīre
pencil	graphium, -ī, n. graphis, graphidis, n.	to pass a test	perītus/a reperīrī
		to receive a grade of A	optimus/a exīstimārī
eraser (for chalk)	spongia, -ae, f.	attend school	scholam frequentāre
eraser (for pencil)	gummis, -is, f.	borrow	mūtuō accipere
clock	hōrologium, -iī, n.	correct a mistake	mendam corrigere
The bell rings.	Tintinnābulum sonat.	correct a student	discipulum castigāre

• Social Interchange •

Hello!	Salvē! Salvēte!	*Come in.*	Ingrediāris; Ingredere
How are you?	Quid agis?	*Did you sleep well?*	Aptē dormīsti?
Are you well?	Ut valēs?	*introduce (one person to another)*	addūcere aliquem
How is it going?	Quid fit?		
I am glad to see you well.	Venīre tē salvum volup est.	*May I introduce Julius to you?*	Liceat tibi addūcere Iūlium? Tuā licentiā ad tē dēdūcō Iūlium.
To greet one another.	Consalutāre inter sē.		
What's going on? How are you getting on?	Quid agitur (fit)?	*Pleased to meet you.*	libenter, libentissimē
Where are you going?	Quō tendis?	*Give him my regards.*	Salvēre illum iube meō nōmine.
I am fine.	Valeō.		
Fine, very fine!	Bene! Perbene!	*Remember me to your brother.*	Nuntiā frātrī tuō salūtem verbīs meīs
Not bad.	Haud male.	*Say hi to your folk.*	Cūrā ut tuōs meīs verbīs salūtēs
Everything's fine.	Omnia sunt rectē.		

See you.	inter nōs revideāmus, usque in proximam vicem /proximum congressum)	*I'm sorry, excuse me, forgive me.*	me excūsātum habeās; ignosce; veniam petō
See you later.	in posterum	*just as you wish*	arbītriō tuō
See you tomorrow.	in crastīnum	*I'm happy to hear that.*	benē narrās (dē ...)
Good bye!	Valē! Valēte! Tē valeō iubeō; valeās; vīve et valē; valē et bene ambulā	*I'm sorry to hear.*	malē narrās (dē ...)
		Your health!	Benē tibi (tē)!
Good luck!	Bene sit tibi! Macte virtūte (estō / tē esse iubeō).	*Cicero sends cordial greetings to Atticus.*	Cicerō Atticō SDP (Salūtem dīcit plurimam)
		Everything depends on you.	In tē omnia sunt.
Have good trip.	bonum iter, benē itinerāre	*That is exactly what I think.*	Ita prorsus existimō.
A safe journey to you.	Benē ambulā et redambulā.	*my fault*	mea culpa, meā culpā
to the extent I am able	quod eius facere possum, quoad in mē est	*To say the least.*	ne(quid) graviūs dīcam.
		I have no objection	Per mē licet.
Well done!	euge, faberrimē factum	*I drink to your health.*	Prōpīnō tibi hoc (pōculum).
What do you do (for a living)?	quō mūnere fungeris? quem locum tenēs?	*to the best of my ability*	quantum in mē (situm) est
You're right.	rectē dīcis (aut monēs)	*it is an open question / undecided (lit. untouched)*	rēs integra est.

• Sport •

Do you wish to play?	Placetne tibi lūdere?	*To play odd or even.*	Lūdere pār impār.
Let's play together.	Inter nōs lūdāmus.	*To learn fencing.*	Discere rudibus.
How much do you bet?	Quā sponsiōne vīs lūdere?	*He fences.*	Rudibus ēlūdit.
To win the bet.	Sponsiōne vincere.	*I give you the game.*	Tibi cēdō.
To challenge someone to play	Lūdō aliquem poscere.	*to play baseball*	pilā clāvāque lūdere; basīpilam lūdere
He is teaching him how to play ball.	Docet eum pilam.	*to play tennis*	tenisiam lūdere
		to play basketball	corbifolle lūdere
To play chess.	Trunculiīs lūdere.	*Whose turn is it?*	Cuius sunt partēs? Ad quem pervēnit? Quis proximus est?

• Time •

What time is it?	Quota hōra est? Quid hōra est?	*at noon*	merīdiē
		sooner or later	sērius ōcius
in the morning	māne	*early, timely*	mātūrē
in the early morning	prīmō māne multō māne	*too late*	sērō
		till a late hour	multō diē

till late at night	ad multam noctem	*the day after tomorrow*	perendiē
every day	singulīs diēbus	*How long?*	Quam diū?
every other day	tertiō quoque diē	*for 4 days*	quattuor diēs
at the beginning of the month	ineunte mense	*How long ago?*	Quam dūdum?
		6 years ago	Abhinc annīs sex
at the end of the month	exeunte mense	*3 months ago*	ante hīs tribus mensibus
		term	terminus, -ī, m.
last week	hebdomas superior hebdomas prior	*spring term*	terminus vernus
		summer term	terminus aestīvus
last year	annus superior annus prior	*fall term*	terminus autumnālis
		holiday	diēs festus
next week	hebdomas proxima	*school day*	diēs scholae
next year	annus proximus	*the first day of classes after vacation*	prīma diēs scholae post fēriās
two days before yesterday	nudius quārtus		
the day before yesterday	nudius tertius	*exam period*	spatium examina subeundī
yesterday	herī		
yesterday's	hesternus, -a, -um	*When is your birthday?*	Quandō tibi nātālis diēs est?
today	hodiē		
today's	hodiernus, -a, -um	*At Christmas*	diē nātālī Christī
tomorrow	crās	*At Easter*	Paschālī tempore
tommorrow's	crāstinus, -a, -um		

• Transport •

to drive	gubernāre; agere	*on foot*	pedibus; crūribus
to ride	vehor, vehī (passive)	*on horse*	in equō
by bicycle	in birotā	*by train*	trāmine
by car	autoraedā; currū	*by plane*	āëroplanō
on camel	in camēlō	*by motorcycle*	in autobirotā
on elephant	in elephantō	*by ship*	nāve

• Various •

Oh, poor me!	Vae miserō mihi!	*Never mind.*	Nōn est operae pretium.
God help us!	Bene vertat deus!	*What did you say?*	Quid dixistī?
I'll cross my fingers.	Pollicem premam.	*Just in case.*	in omnem eventum
No sooner said than done.	Dīctum ac factum.	*in many respects*	multīs rebus (locīs)
My stomach grumbles.	Vacuus mihi venter crepitat.	*a favorable opportunity presents itself*	occāsīo dātur (offertur)
Bon appetit!	Sit fēlix convīvium.	*Experience has taught me.*	ūsus mē docuit.
Over wine	per vīnum		
My condolences.	Tibi condolēscō.		

• Latin Phrases in Modern Use •

ā fortiorī.	*from the stronger; even more so; with even stronger reason.*
ā posse ad esse.	*from possibility to actuality.*
ā posteriorī.	*derived by reasoning from observed facts.*
ā priorī.	*from what was before.*
ab incunablis.	*from the origin; from the cradle.*
ab initiō.	*from the beginning.*
ab urbe condita (AUC).	*from the founding of the city (Rome in 753 BC).*
ad absurdum.	*to the point of absurdity.*
ad hoc.	*for this special purpose.*
ad hominem.	*to the man, a personal attack.*
ad hominem.	*appealing to feelings rather than reason.*
ad idem.	*of the same mind.*
ad infīnītum.	*without limit.*
ad libitum.	*according to pleasure.*
ad lītem.	*for the suit.*
ad nauseam.	*to a disgusting extent.*
ad valōrem.	*according to value.*
addenda.	*things to be added.*
advocātus diabolī.	*devil's advocate.*
affidavit.	*a sworn written statement usable as evidence in court.*
agenda.	*things to be done (used especially for a list of items to be discussed at a meeting).*
ālea iacta est.	*the die is cast (Caesar).*
alibī.	*elsewhere.*
alma māter.	*one's old school or university.*
alter ego.	*other self.*
amīcus cūriae.	*friend of the court.*
amīcus omnibus, amīcus neminī.	*a friend to all is a friend to none.*

annō dominī (AD).	*in the year of the Lord.*
annus horribilis.	*a terrible year.*
annus mīrābilis.	*a wonderful year.*
ante bellum.	*before the war.*
ante merīdiem (a.m.).	*before midday.*
aqua pūra.	*pure water.*
aqua vītae	*alcohol.*
ars grātiā artis.	*art for art's sake.*
audē sapere.	*dare know.*
bonā fidē (adjective).	*genuine, sincere.*
bona fides (noun).	*honest intention.*
cadit quaestiō (cq).	*the question falls; the matter has been resolved.*
carpe diem.	*Seize the day. Live fully*
cāsus bellī.	*The justification for war.*
cave canem.	*Beware of the dog.*
caveat emptor.	*Let the buyer beware.*
caveat lector.	*Let the reader beware.*
caveat venditor.	*Let the seller beware.*
cēterīs paribus	*all other things being equal*
circā (c. and followed by a date).	*about.*
cōgitō, ergō sum.	*I think, therefore I am (Descartes).*
compos mentis.	*of sound mind; sane.*
confer (cf.).	*compare.*
corpus dēlictī.	*the facts of a crime.*
corrigenda.	*a list of things to be corrected (in a book).*
cui bonō?	*who benefits?*
cui malō?	*who suffers a detriment?*
cum grānō salis.	*with a grain of salt (that is, not literally).*
curriculum vītae.	*an outline of a person's career.*
dē factō.	*in fact (as opposed to "dē jure").*
dē gustibus nōn est disputandum.	*there is no accounting for taste.*

dē jure.	*by right (as opposed to "de facto").*
dē minimīs (nōn cūrat lēx).	*with respect to trifles; the law is not interested in trivial matters.*
dē novō.	*anew.*
deō dūce.	*with God for a leader.*
deō grātiās.	*thanks be to God.*
deō volente.	*God willing.*
deus ex māchinā.	*a contrived event that resolves a problem (literally, "a god from a machine").*
dictum meum pactum.	*my word is my bond.*
dictum sapientī sat est.	*a word to the wise is sufficient.*
docendō discimus.	*We learn by teaching.*
drāmatis persōnae.	*a list of characters in a play.*
dulce et decōrum est prō pātriā morī.	*it is sweet and proper to die for one's country (Horace).*
dum spīrō, spērō.	*as long as I breathe, I hope (Cicero).*
dūrā lēx, sed lēx.	*the law is harsh, but it is the law.*
ecce homō.	*behold the man.*
eiusdem generis.	*of the same kind.*
ēmeritus.	*retired after distinguished service and holding an honorary title (for example, emeritus professor).*
ergō.	*therefore.*
errāta.	*a list of errors (in a book).*
et alia.	*and other things.*
et aliī (et al.).	*and others.*
et cetera (etc.).	*and so on.*
et sequentēs (et seq. or seqq.).	*and those that follow.*
et uxor (et ux.).	*and wife.*

ex cathēdrā.	*(of a pronouncement) formally, with official authority.*
ex cūriā.	*out of court.*
ex grātiā.	*purely as a favour.*
ex librīs.	*from the library of.*
ex nihilō.	*out of nothing.*
ex officiō.	*by virtue of his office.*
ex parte.	*by only one party to a dispute in the absence of the other.*
ex post facto.	*retrospectively.*
exeat.	*permission for a temporary absence.*
exemplī grātiā (e.g.).	*for example.*
fāmā nihil est celerius.	*nothing is swifter than a rumour.*
fīat.	*let it be done.*
flōruit.	*he flourished.*
functus officiō.	*having discharged his duty and thus ceased to have any authority over a matter.*
gaudeāmus igitur.	*so let us rejoice.*
habeās corpus.	*you may have the body. (requiring a person holding another person to bring that person before a court.)*
hīc jacet.	*here lies.*
honōris causā.	*as a mark of esteem.*
ibidem (ibid. in citations of books, etc.).	*in the same place.*
id est (i.e.).	*that is.*
īdem.	*the same.*
imprimātur.	*let it be printed.*
in absentiā.	*while absent.*
in camerā.	*in private session.*
in cāsū extrēmae necessitātis.	*in case of extreme necessity.*
in cāsū.	*in this case.*
in cūria.	*in court.*
in extrēmīs.	*near death.*

in flāgrante dēlictō.	*in the very act of committing an offence.*	magnum opus.	*A great work.*
in illō tempore.	*at that time.*	manus manum lavat.	*the hand washes the hand; returning a favor.*
in locō parentīs.	*in place of a parent.*	mē jūdice.	*With me as judge; in my opinion*
in mediās rēs.	*into the midst of things.*	meā culpā.	*by my fault (used as an acknowledgement of one's error).*
in memoriam.	*in memory.*		
in rē.	*in the matter of.*	mementō morī.	*Be mindful of death.*
in silicō.	*by means of a computer simulation.*	memorandum.	*A thing to be remembered.*
in sitū.	*in its original situation.*	mens rea.	*guilty mind.*
in speciē.	*in kind; in its own form and not in an equivalent.*	mens sāna in corpore sānō.	*a sound mind in a sound body.*
in tōtō.	*entirely.*	mīrābile dīctu.	*wonderful to relate.*
in vīnō verītās.	*in wine there is truth.*	modus operandī.	*the manner of working.*
in vītrō.	*in a glass test tube; outside the living body.*	multum in parvō.	*much in a small compass.*
in vīvō.	*happening within a living organism.*	multus amīcus, nullus amīcus.	*a friend to all is a friend to none.*
infrā.	*below or on a later page.*	mūtātīs mūtandīs.	*the necessary changes being made.*
inter alia.	*among other things.*	nē plus ultra.	*the highest standard of excellence.*
inter sē.	*among themselves.*	nemine dissentiente. (nem. dis.)	*unanimously.*
inter vīvōs.	*during life.*		
intra mūrōs.	*within the walls.*	nihil obstat.	*nothing stands in the way.*
intra vīrēs.	*within the power.*	nil dēspērandum.	*there is no cause for despair (Horace).*
ipsō factō.	*by that very fact.*		
lapsus linguae.	*a slip of the tongue.*	nīsī.	*unless.*
locō citātō (loc. cit.).	*in the passage just quoted.*	nōlēns volēns.	*whether one likes it or not; willing or unwilling.*
locum tenēns.	*a person who temporarily fulfills the duties of another; a deputy.*	nolle prōsequi.	*to be unwilling to prosecute.*
locus sigillī (l.s.).	*the place of the seal.*	nōlō contendēre.	*I do not wish to contend (the charges).*
locus standī.	*the right to be heard in court.*	nōn compos mentis.	*insane.*
magna carta.	*Great Charter (issued by King John in 1215, limiting his power, notably with habeas corpus).*	nōn sequitur.	*it does not follow.*
		notā bene (NB).	*note well.*
magnā cum laude.	*With great honour.*	ō tempora, ō morēs!	*oh, the times! oh, the morals! (Cicero).*

obiter dīctum.	*said in passing. A legal term for non-binding comments added by a judge to a court decision.*
omne ignōtum prō magnificō est.	*all things unknown seem grand (Tacitus the Elder).*
omnia mūtantur, nōs et mūtāmur in illīs.	*all things are changing, and we are changing with them.*
omnia vincit amor, nōs et cēdāmus amōrī.	*love conquers all things, let us too yield to love (Virgil).*
opere citātō (op. cit.).	*in the work just quoted.*
parī passū.	*equally.*
parturiunt montēs, nascētur rīdiculus mūs.	*A lot of hot air; useless outcome (literally, "the mountains are in labour; a ridiculous mouse will be born") (Horace).*
passim.	*in various places (in a quoted work).*
pāx intrantibus.	*peace to those who enter.*
pāx vōbiscum.	*peace be with you.*
pendente līte.	*pending the suit.*
per annum.	*per year.*
per ardua ad alta.	*through difficulties to the heights.*
per ardua ad astra.	*through difficulties to the stars.*
per capita.	*by the head.*
per centum.	*per hundred.*
per diem.	*per day.*
per mensem.	*per month.*
per omnia saecula saeculōrum.	*for ever and ever.*
per sē.	*by itself.*
persōna nōn grāta.	*a non-acceptable person.*
post hoc ergō propter hoc.	*after this, therefore because of this; a logical fallacy.*
post merīdiem (p.m.).	*after midday.*
post mortem.	*after death (also figuratively).*
prīmā faciē.	*on a first view.*
prīmus inter parēs.	*first among equals.*
prō bonō pūblicō.	*in the public good.*
prō bonō.	*done without charge.*
prō formā.	*for the sake of form.*
prō hāc vice.	*for this occasion.*
prō ratā.	*according to the rate.*
prō sē.	*on one's own behalf.*
prō tantō.	*to that extent.*
prō tempore (pro tem).	*for the time being.*
proximō (prox.).	*of the next month.*
quantum in mē fuit.	*I have done my best.*
quasi.	*as if.*
quī dēsīderat pācem, prāeparet bellum.	*let him who desires peace prepare for war (Vegetius).*
quid prō quō.	*something for something.*
quis custōdiet ipsōs cūstodēs?	*who is guarding the guards?*
quō in casū.	*in which case.*
quō vādis?	*where are you going?*
quod erat dēmonstrandum (QED).	*which was to be proved.*
quod vidē (q.v.).	*which see.*
ratiō dēcidendī.	*the reason for the decision.*
ratiō lēgis est anima lēgis.	*the reason of the law is the soul of the law.*
rē.	*in the matter of; concerning.*
reductiō ad absurdum.	*reduction to the absurd.*
requiescat in pāce.	*rest in peace.*
rēs ipsa loquitur.	*the thing speaks for itself.*
rigor mortis.	*the stiffening of a body after death.*
semel in annō licet insānīre.	*one can act the fool once a year.*

semper fidēlis.	*always faithful.*	sub rōsā.	*in confidence.*
senātus populusque Rōmānus (SPQR).	*the Senate and the people of Rome.*	suī generis.	*of its own kind.*
		sūprā.	*above or on an earlier page.*
sensū strictō.	*in a narrow or strict sense.*	suum cuique.	*to each his own.*
seqq.	*and those that follow.*	tempus fugit.	*time flies.*
seriatim.	*one after another in order.*	terra firma.	*dry land.*
		terra incognita.	*unknown land.*
si vīs pācem, parā bellum.	*if you want peace, prepare for war.*	terra nullius.	*uninhabited land.*
sīc transit glōria mundī.	*thus passes the glory of the world.*	timeō danaōs et dōna ferentēs.	*I fear the Greeks, even bearing gifts (Virgil).*
sīc.	*thus (used in quoted passages to indicate that an error has been deliberately reproduced).*	ultimō (ult.).	*of the previous month.*
		ultrā vīrēs.	*beyond the power.*
		vāde mēcum.	*a constant companion.*
		velle est posse.	*where there is a will, there is a way.*
silentium est aureum.	*silence is golden.*	vēnī, vīdī, vīcī.	*I came, I saw, I conquered (Caesar).*
silva rērum.	*an assorted collection of facts.*	verbatim.	*word for word; exactly as said.*
simpliciter.	*naturally; without qualification.*	verbum sat sapientī . (verb. sap.)	*a word to the wise is sufficient.*
sine annō (s.a.).	*year not known.*	versus.	*against.*
sine diē.	*without a day decided.*	vī et armīs.	*by force and arms.*
sine quā nōn.	*an indispensable condition.*	vice versā.	*the order being reversed.*
status quō.	*the existing conditionor situation.*	vidē.	*see.*
		vidēlicet (viz.).	*namely.*
stet.	*let it stand (used in editing to indicate that something crossed out is to remain).*	vīva voce.	*orally, with the living voice.*
		vox populī.	*voice of the people.*
sub jūdice.	*before a court.*		

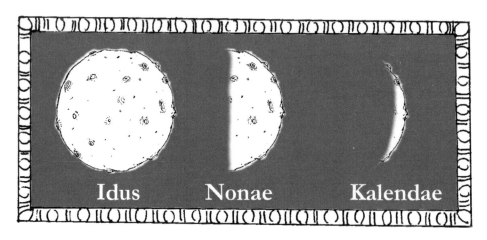

Idus   Nonae   Kalendae

At its beginning, the Roman system of time-keeping was lunar. A priest was entrusted with the duty of tracking the moon. When he saw the first sliver of a cresent moon, he would declare the new month by calling it out. The Latin word for solemnly calling or summoning is *calo, calare*. From this custom, the word "Kalendae" was born and so our word "calendar". The day of Kalends each month is dedicated to Juno, the Ides to Jupiter.

We now familiarize ourselves with the Roman Calendar mainly for the enjoyment of reading monuments or official documents. Being able to write the date the Roman way will add a dash of erudition to even the humblest of your documents. A PDF file is available on this book's websites with all the dates fully written out. Alternatively, the American Classical League publishes a Roman calendar each year.

Dates are usually abbreviated in writing and with good reason! Here is a list of abbreviations:

$$\begin{array}{rcl}
\textit{ante diem} & - & \textit{a.d.} \\
\textit{Kalendas, Kalendis} & - & \textit{Kal.} \\
\textit{Nonas, Nonis} & - & \textit{Non.} \\
\textit{Idus, Idibus} & - & \textit{Id.}
\end{array}$$

Numbers were naturally written in Roman numerals. A date such as March 4th is *ante diem quartum Nonas Martias*. It would be written: *a.d. IV Non. Mar.*

These date expressions are treated as nouns, just add the prepostions *ad, in* (up to) or *ex* (from). e.g.: *ex a.d. IV Non. Mar.* – from March 4th or *in a.d. IV Non. Mar.* – up to March 4th.

For further information on this fascinating subject and other calendars of the world please visit this web site: http://www.webexhibits.org/calendars/calendar-roman.html

APPENDIX V NUMBERS

Arabic	Roman	CARDINAL *quot?* how many?	ORDINAL *quotus?* which in order?	DISTRIBUTIVE *quotēni?* how many each?	ADVERBS *quotien (quotiēs)?* how many times / often?
1	I	ūnus (ūna, ūnam)	prīmus (-a, -um)	singulī (-ae, -a)	semel
2	II	duo (duae, duo)	secundus, alter	bīnī	bis
3	III	trēs (trēs, tria)	tertius	ternī	ter
4	IV	quattuor	quārtus	quaternī	quater
5	V	quīnque	quīntus	quīnī	quīnquiē(n)s
6	VI	sex	sextus	sēnī	sexiēns
7	VII	septem	septimus	septēnī	septiēns
8	VIII	octō	octāvus	octōni	octiēns
9	IX	novem	nōnus	novēnī	noviēns
10	X	decem	decimus	dēnī	deciēns
11	XI	ūndecim	ūndecimus	ūndēnī	ūndeciēns
12	XII	duodecim	duodecimus	dodēnī	duodeciēns
13	XIII	trēdecim	tertius decimus	ternī dēnī	terdeciēns
14	XIV	quattuordecim	quārtus decimus	quaternī dēnī	quaterdeciēns
15	XV	quīndecim	quīntus decimus	quīnī dēnī	quīndeciēns
16	XVI	sēdecim	sextus decimus	sēdenī dēnī	sēdeciēns
17	XVII	septendecim	septimus decimus	septenī dēnī	septiēns deciēns
18	XVIII	duodēvīgintī	duodēvīcē(n)simus	duodēvīcēnī	duodēvīciēns
19	XIX	ūndēvīgintī	ūndēvīcēnsimus	ūndēvīcēnī	ūndēvīciēns
20	XX	vīgintī	vīcēnsimus	vīcēnī	vīciēns
21	XXI	ūnus et vīgintī	ūnus et vīcēnsimus	vīcēnī singulī	semel et vīciēns
30	XXX	trīgintā	trīcēnsimus	trīcēnī	trīciēns
40	XL	quadrāgintā	quadrāgēnsimus	quadrāgēnī	quadrāgiēns
50	L	quīnquāgintā	quīnquāgēnsimus	quīnquāgēnī	quīnquāgiēns
60	LX	sexāgintā	sexāgēnsimus	sexāgēnī	sexāgiēns
70	LXX	septuāgintā	septuāgēnsimus	septuāgēnī	septuāgiēns
80	LXXX	octōgintā	octōgēnsimus	octōgēnī	octōgiēns
90	XC	nōnāgintā	nōnāgēnsimus	nōnāgēnī	nōnāgiēns
100	C	centum	centēnsimus	centēnī	centiēns
200	CC	ducentī, -ae, -a	ducentēnsimus	ducēnī	ducentiēns
300	CCC	trecentī	trecentēsimus	trecēnī	trecentiēs
400	CCCC	quadringentī	quadringentēsimus	quadringēnī	quadringentiēs

Arabic	Roman	CARDINAL *quot?* how many?	ORDINAL *quotus?* which in order?	DISTRIBUTIVE *quotēni?* how many each?	ADVERBS *quotien (quotiēs)?* how many times / often?
500	D	quīngentī	quīngentēsimus	quīngēnī	quīngentiēs
600	DC	sescentī	sescentēsimus	sescēnī	sescentiēs
700	DCC	septingentī	septingentēsimus	septingēnī	septingentiēs
800	DCCC	octingentī	octingentēsimus	octingēnī	octingentiēs
900	DCCCC	nōngentī	nongentēnsimus	nōngēnī	nōngentiēns
1000	M	mīlle	mīllēnsimus	mīllēnī	mīlliēns
2000	MM	duo mīlia	bīs mīllēnsimus	bīna mīlia	bis mīlliēns
100,000	C̄	centum mīlia	centiēs mīllēsimus	centēna mīlia	centiēs mīliēs
1,000,000	M̄	deciēs centēna mīlia	deciēs centiēs mīllēsimus	deciēs centēna mīlia	deciēs centiēs mīliēs

Cardinals from *quattuor* to *centum* are indeclinable; from *ducentī* to *nōngentī* they are declined like the standard first and second declension plural adjectives. *Mīlle* in the singular is an indeclinable noun or adjective; the plural *mīlia* is a neuter noun declined like *tria*.

> *mīlle modīs*, in a thousand ways.
> *cum mīlle hominibus*, with a thousand men.
> *mīlle trahēns variōs colōrēs* (Aen. iv. 701), drawing out a thousand various colors.

Ordinals are declined like the standard first and second declension adjectives. The letter "n" is often ommitted in forming ordinal numbers in -ensimus.

The Ordinals must be used to give the years:
> A.D. 100 is *annō post Christum nātō centēnsimō*.
> "in the year 2009" is *annō bis mīllēsimō nōnō*.

Distributives are declined like the standard first and second declension plural adjectives. Its uses:

(a) denotes that the number belongs to each of several persons or things, as *puerī dēn(ōr)um annōrum*, boys of ten years old; *singula singulīs*, one apiece (one each to each one); *agrī septēna iūgera plēbī dīvīsa sunt*, i.e. seven jugera to each citizen (seven jugera each), *bīna talenta eīs dedit,* he gave them two talents each.

(b) are used in multiplication, as *bis bīna sunt quattuor,* twice two are four; *ter septēnīs diēbus*, in thrice seven days.

(c) with nouns which have no corresponding singular, such as *ūna castra*, one camp, but *bīna castra*, two camps (*duo castra* would mean two forts), and *bīnae litterae*, two epistles, but *duae litterae*, two letters of the alphabet; and

(d) poets often use distributives for cardinals particularly where pairs or sets are spoken of: as, *bīna hastīlia*, two spears (two in a set).

Units	I	II	III	IV	V	VI	VII	VIII	IX
Tens	X	XX	XXX	XL	L	LX	LXX	LXXX	XC
Hundreds	C	CC	CCC	CD	D	DC	DCC	DCCC	CM
Thousands	M	MM	MMM	ĪV	V̄	V̄I	V̄II	V̄III	ĪX

APPENDIX VI GRAMMAR NOTES & ACTIVITIES

Grammatical Notes

The grammatical notes are largely limited to the main conversation. For more in depth explanations, teachers are directed to Allen & Greenough's <u>New Latin Grammar</u> which is widely available on the internet, or in print form from Focus Publishing (www.pullins.com). A reference will appear in this way: **NLG 427**. This would direct you to section 427 of the grammar (*not* the page number).

Activities

You might find these helpful in planning your lessons and learning. Immediately below are some activities that can be applied to almost every conversation:

Walk & Talk: Just as the name suggests, get students out of their seats and moving around. It can be organized in a few ways.

- Make 2 lines, A and B. Students perform the dialogue. The person at the end of line B shifts over to line A and the person at the head of line A shifts over to line B. Thus, a rotation is achieved. Every student will eventually perform both sides of the conversation.
- Make 2 lines, A and B. Students perform the dialogue. The person at the end of line B moves to the head of line B and everyone in that line shifts over. Students only need to perform one side of the dialogue.
- Make 2 concentric circles. Inner is A, the outer is B. The outer rotates after performing the dialogue. Students need only perform one side of the dialogue.
- Random. You may wish to specify how many partners the students must perform with. They may even be asked to keep notes. Students can play *odd-even* or *rock, scissors, paper* to decide who goes first.

It may help to signal to the students when they should change partners by clapping, whistling or ringing a bell. Students should then make closure and move; e.g. A: "Oh! Tempus est! Numquid vis?" B: "Ut valeas."

Disappearing Text: This can be used in conjunction with *Walk & Talk*. First, write the dialogue on the black board, leaving blanks for the parts that vary. Write the variations on the board as well or have students keep a note handy. Students perform the dialogue, freely looking at the board whenever they need. Then, the teacher erases a word or two (or parts of words). Students perform the dialogue again, relying on their memory for the missing parts. Again the teacher erases some parts. Continue until the entire dialogue is gone.

Build it up: Take two conversations and put them together using a conversation gambit (see the vocabulary appendix), such as; *by the way, let me change the subject* etc.

Finally, more ideas, notes and printable resources can be found on the author's and publisher's sites: **www.discamus.com** & **http://courses.pullins.com**

Unit	Grammar Points	Activities
1	*Salve*: imperative (plural is *Salvete*). NLG 448.	Walk & Talk; Disappearing text. (see previous page)
2	*Velim*: 1st person singular subjunctive (optative). NLG 442 b. *Marce*: vocative. NLG 35.	Give each student a picture of a famous person (or they can bring / draw pictures of family and friends. Use these for the person being inroduced. Walk & Talk; Disappearing Text.
3	*(Ex) Italia*: ablative of place from which. Towns, small islands, *domus* & *rus* without prepostion. NLG 427.	Give each student a card with a city prompt on one side (role A) and a country and different city prompt on the other side (role B). Students then use these for Walk & Talk; Disappearing Text.
4	See appendix on numbers.	• Dictate numbers to students. • Prepare information on a number of historical / current popular individuals (cross curricular opportunity) and use it for this dialogue. • Teacher says the answer and students give the question; e.g. T: *"Tulius."* SS: *"Quid est praenomen tuum?"*
5	*-ne*: question. NLG 332. *Novo Eboraco*: ablative of place from which. NLG 427.	see Lesson 3
6	See appendix on numbers. *Ignosce*: imperative (plural: *Ignoscite*). *mihi*: dative with the verb of pardon. NLG 367.	see Lesson 4
7	*telephonice*: ablative of means. NLG 409. *vocabo*: 1st person future indicative active.	Place pictures of buildings around the room. Ask students to stand under them. Then "call" a student and ask for individuals not at that location.
8	*Marce*: vocative NLG 35. *ignosce mihi*: see lesson 6. *Noli*: imperative (plural *nolite*), with the infinitive it means "don't". NLG 450 *sollicitari*: present passive infinitive, literally "to be worried". *valeas*: 2nd person singular present subjunctive NLG 441.	"Call" students at their seats. It may help to give each student a card with an activity printed or pictured on it. Place the cards around the room for students to stand under, if you like.
9	See appendix on numbers. *Mihi eundum est*: passive pariphrastic. NLG 500. *Opus est*: literally, "There is need", with the infinitive and dative it means "I need to.." *conveniamus*: 1st person pl. present subjuctive. NLG 441.	Write a simple schedule on the board with activities for each hour. Have students take turns randomly calling out the time to which you resond, *"Opus est mihi ....!"*. You can also place pictures of activies around the room and move to them.

104

10	*Quota hora*: ablative of time. NLG 423. *incipiet*: 3rd person singular future active. *Secunda hora*: ablative of time when. *Nobis festinandum est.*: passive pariphrastic. NLG 500.	Quiz the students in Latin about their class schedule. Ask about what time TV programs and events start.
11	*(Possumne) -ne*: question. NLG 332. See appendix on numbers. *emas*: 2nd person singular subjunctive. NLG 439. *Quaeso*: can also appear with the imperative or *ut / ne* + subjunctive.	The long shopping list: A student begins, "I'm going to the store to buy..." and adds an item. The next student repeats the line (including the previous student's item) and adds his own. Continue until someone misses an item. (Keep notes! Conduct disputes *Latine*.)
12	*Quo*: adverb of place, "To what place?" *ad* + accusative; towns, small islands, *domus* & *rus* without prepostion. NLG 427.	Place pictures of buildings around the room. Ask students to decide on a place to go (it may be advisable to pass out destination cards) and meet at least three people on the way to their destination. You can ask them to keep a note on scrap paper and quiz them later.
13	*licet*: impersonal verb "it is allowed" + dative and infinitive. NLG 208 c, 368, 454. It may also take the subjunctive. NLG 565.	A version of "Simon says" or "Mother, may I?" would be appropriate.
14	*Ignosce mihi*: see unit 6. *iuxta, inter, exadversum* + accusative. *exadversum* alternatively *exadversus*.	• The five conversations in this unit create the layout of a street. Ask students to draw a map. • On the board, draw a simple map and quiz students, "What's next to..." "What's opposite..." Then have students work in pairs or small groups to describe a street to their partners. Having small pictures of buildings will help. • Printable pictures of buildings available on this book's websites.
15	*vidisti-ne*: 2nd person singular perfect (*video*). *in mediano*: for a list of prepositions see NLG 220, 221.	Collect objects from students and put them in a bag. Randomly pull them out and ask various students, "Is this your ...?"
16	*opus est mihi*: "I need ...+ ablative. NLG 411. *illic*: for a list of adverbs of place see NLG 217.	Set up the classroom like a shop, placing objects (or pictures) around. Then tell students what you're looking for.
17	*Constat* + ablative of price NLG 417. *Ostende*: imperative singular (plural is *ostendite*) + direct object (accusative) and indirect object (dative).	Ask students "*Ostendite mihi ....*" + desktop objects, hands, nose, etc. Then, students can ask you "*Ostende nobis...*".
18	*Iste, ista, istud*: NLG 297 c. *Laetissimus*: superlative adjective NLG 124.	Write a number of adjectives on the board. Then hold up items and announce, "*nūper ___ ēmi!*" Students then respond with an adjective of their choosing.

19	*caletur*: 3rd person singular deponent present. *visne*: 2nd person singular present active (*volo*) + infinitive. NLG 563 b. *natemus*: 3rd person plural present subjunctive (horatory). NLG 439.	Draw a grid on the board and write different types of weather at the top of each column. Then discuss with the class what sort of activities are possible or suitable for each type of weather.
20	*una*: an adverb from unus. This dialogue has the same grammar as unit 19 plus the perfect indicative (e.g. *natavimus*)	Walk & Talk; Disappearing text.
21	*hac nocte*: ablative of time when. NLG 423. *telephonice*: ablative of means (see unit 7). *in theatro eram*: imperfect tense because the speaker was present for a continuous time in the past.	Make a schedule of hours on the board. Students then ask you what you were doing the previous Sunday at each hour and you answer, writing it next to the time. Students make their own schedules, filling in the activities. Then you call on them. As pair work, students can interview each other.
22	*ages*: 2nd person singular future indicative. *ad forum emptum ibo.*: eo + the supine in "-um" expresses purpose. NLG 509. *ad meridiem*: NLG 424 e.	Make a fortune-teller by folding a piece of paper. Use it to practice the future tense. (See this book's website for more details and instructions.)
23	*egisti*: 2nd person singular perfect active (*ago*). *videtur*: 3rd person singular present passive. It often appears with the dative (e.g. *mihi*). NLG 375 b.	Try to guess what students did last night / yesterday. Pair students up and ask them to list at least 5 things they both did yesterday.
24	*cura*: imperative (plural *curate*). *cura* + *ut* & subjunctive: NLG 449 c.	Walk & Talk; Disappearing text.
25	*videris*: 2nd person singular present passive "You seem" (see *videtur* unit 23). *quod discipuli ...*: quod + indicative: NLG 540. *quia* is also acceptable.	Write a list of common Latin expressions on the board. Then assign students a feeling at random and ask them to read the saying with that emotion.
26	*Mavis-ne*: 2nd person singular present from *malo*. NLG 199. *māla*: neuter plural. Not to be confused with *malus, -a, -um*: bad, evil.	Ask student to make a survey of class prefrences. Later they can present the results on a poster, or orally.
27	*Edas-ne*: 2nd person singular present subjunctive (Optative). NLG 441. *foris*: defective noun. NLG 103 c. 4. NLG 427 a.	Create a menu for your class. See the vocabulary appendix.
28	*illīc*: adverb, "there". From *ille*. *Quaenam*: quae + nam. Emphatic. NLG 148 c. *alba ianua*: ablative of quality. NLG 415 a.	• Picture Dictation: Describe some simple buildings and people for your students to draw. "A man with a big nose and three eyes." • Repeat it if it's True: Make statements about a picture. If it's true, students should repeat it.

29	*Uteris-ne*: 2nd person singular active (deponent). *utor, uti* requires the ablative of the object used, here *interrete*. *sodes* (*si audes*), is a friendly form of request. Variations 3 and 4 have indirect speech and so use the subjunctive. NLG 577. *vīcerit*: perfect subjunctive. The main verb is a primary tense and the action is completed. NLG 482.	Use the Latin alphabet to play "Hangman".
30	*velis*: 2nd person singular active (*volo*). *fieri*: infinitive (*fio*) this verb serves as the passive of *facio*. NLG 204. *olim*: adverb, "at some time" either in the past or future. *medicus*: nominative + infinitive. NLG 458.	Create some characters with simple drawings or pictures clipped from magazines. Describe to students what each character likes to do. Then students can tell you what job the character should pursue.
31	*visne* + infinitive; see lesson 19. *Die Solis:* ablative (*die*) of time when. NLG 423.	Conversations 31 - 35 form a cohesive story. They would make a nice short performance to video-tape and share.
32	*intres*: 2nd person singular present subjunctive (horatory). NLG 439. *quaeso*: see unit 11. *esto*: 2nd person singular future imperative (*sum, esse*). *Memento* is the same form. *bibe*: 2nd person singular imperative. *Quam*: adverb "How, to what degree". *Age*: 2nd person singular imperative ("Come!"). *ut domi suae sis*: substantantive clause of purpose. NLG 563 e.	Walk & Talk; Disappearing text.
33	*vocatur*: 3rd person singular present passive *quae*: nominative neuter plural, "What things?" *addita sunt*: 3rd person plural perfect passive.	Many of the dishes in this unit are from Apicius' *De Re Coquinaria*. See the vocabulary appendix for more information.
34	*Scisne*: "Do you know..." following this is indirect discourse. NLG 577. *interfectum iri*: future passive infinitive "will be killed." The active form; *interfecurum esse*. *verone*: *vero* + *ne*, "Really?" *me certiorem fecit*: "He made me more certain." i.e. "He informed me."	Walk & Talk; Disappearing text.
35	*mihi eundum est*: see unit 9. *iamne*: *iam* + *ne*; "Now? Already?" *Audivi ...*: indirect discourse. NLG 577.	Walk & Talk; Disappearing text.

APPENDIX VII   RESOURCES

Printed Texts

Capellanus, Georg (trans Peter Needham) *Latin Can be Fun*. New York, NY: Barnes & Noble Books, 1996

Egger, C. *Lexicon nominum virorum et mulierum*. Rome: Studium, 1957.

Egger, C. *Lexicon nominum locorum*. Rome: Officina Libraria Vaticana, 1977.

Egger, C. *Lexicon recentis latinitatis*. Rome: Officina Libraria Vaticana, 1992-1997.

Helfer, C. *Lexicon auxiliare: ein deutsch-lateinisches Wörterbuch*. Saarbrücken: Societas Latina, 1991

Lebet, Philip E. & Perry, David J. *Vocabula Et Sermones*. The American Classical League, 1981.

Porter W. David (Gwara, Scott Ed.) *Anglo-Saxon Conversations*. The Boydell Press, 1997

Smith, W. and T.D. Hall. *Smith's English-Latin Dictionary*. Wauconda, IL: Bolchazy-Carducci, 2000: repr.

Traupman, John C. *Conversational Latin for Oral Proficiency*. Illinois: Bolchazy-Carducci Publishers, 2004.

Electronic

Communities:
http://avitus.alcuinus.net/scl/   http://www.grexlat.com/index.asp
http://www.vatican.va/roman_curia/institutions_connected/latinitas/documents/index_lt.htm

Neo-Latin word list:
http://wredmond.home.texas.net   http://alpha.furman.edu/~dmorgan/
http://www.vatican.va/roman_curia/institutions_connected/latinitas/documents/rc_latinitas_20040601_lexicon_it.html

Classical Dictionaries:
http://www.nd.edu/~archives/latgramm.htm   http://www.perseus.tufts.edu/cgi-bin/enggreek?lang=la

Encyclopædia:
http://la.wikipedia.org/wiki/Pagina_prima

Names of Places
http://www.columbia.edu/acis/ets/Graesse/contents.html
http://www.lib.byu.edu/~catalog/people/rlm/latin/names.htm
http://en.wikipedia.org/wiki/Latin_names_of_cities

General:
http://www.thelatinlibrary.com/

Please check the web pages below for updates, ideas and printable materials.

Author's site:
http://www.discamus.com/
http://www.perlingua.com/

Publisher site: *on-line course*
http://www.pullins.com/   courses.pullins.com